JUSTICES OF THE PEACE

OF

COLONIAL VIRGINIA

1757-1775

EDWARD INGLE

JANAWAY PUBLISHING, INC.
SANTA MARIA, CALIFORNIA
2011

Notice

In many older books, foxing (or discoloration) occurs and, in some instances, print lightens with wear and age. Reprinted books, such as this, often duplicate these flaws, notwithstanding efforts to reduce or eliminate them. The pages of this reprint have been digitally enhanced and, where possible, the flaws eliminated in order to provide clarity of content and a pleasant reading experience.

Originally issued in the *Bulletin of the Virginia State Library*, Volume XIV, Numbers 2 and 3, April, July, 1921.

Originally Published:
Richmond:
1922

Reprinted by:

Janaway Publishing, Inc.
732 Kelsey Ct.
Santa Maria, California 93454
(805) 925-1038
www.janawaygenealogy.com

2011

ISBN: 978-1-59641-236-1

Bulletin of the Virginia State Library

(Issued Quarterly)

Edited by H. R. McILWAINE, State Librarian

| VOL. XIV. | APRIL, JULY, 1921 | Nos. 2, 3 |

JUSTICES OF THE PEACE

OF

COLONIAL VIRGINIA

1757-1775

RICHMOND:

DAVIS BOTTOM, SUPERINTENDENT PUBLIC PRINTING

1922

State Library Board of Virginia

State Library Staff

Publisher's Preface

This book has been excerpted from the *Bulletin of the Virginia State Library* (Issued Quarterly), Volume XIX, Nos. 2 and 3, April, July, 1921; by H. R. McIlwaine, State Librarian, Published 1922, and includes numbered pages 41 to 149 of the original volume. This work retains those original page numbers.

Janaway Publishing, Inc.

Bulletin of the Virginia State Library

(Issued Quarterly)

Edited by H. R. McILWAINE, State Librarian

| Vol. XIV. | APRIL, JULY, 1921 | Nos. 2, 3. |

INTRODUCTORY NOTE.

The manuscript record here printed for the first time was deposited in the archival annex of the Virginia State Library some months ago, with other manuscript material, by the Hon. Charles A. Johnston, State Treasurer, for safe-keeping. It appears to be a record kept for convenience in the period immediately preceding the Revolutionary War by that official whom it most concerned to have at hand a list of all the justices of the peace of the various counties of colonial Virginia. This official was probably the Secretary of the Colony, whose duty it was to issue commissions to the justices, or it may possibly have been the clerk of the Executive Council, who acted also, no doubt, as the clerk of the Governor. Though the commissions were prepared by the Secretary of the Colony, or in his office, they were signed by the Governor, who had the right of appointment, with and by the advice of the Council.

Whether, however, originally made in the office of the Secretary of the Council or in that of the Secretary of the Colony, the record is undoubtedly an authentic one, and it is, for the later entries at least, contemporary with the issuance of the commissions recorded. It may be relied upon as being accurate. From this arises its peculiar value.

The aim has been to publish the manuscript exactly as it is, except for the check-marks which frequently appear in front of the names. The reproduction of these did not seem to be at all essential. All the notations, such as "dead," "removed," "out of country," etc., are printed accurately, since they give information. Both in the interests of accuracy and as a reminder of the age of the manuscript, even the abbreviations appearing in the original are given as nearly as can be done by the use merely of usual modern type. For the sake of the references made in the preface, the page numbers of the manuscript are indicated.

The preface has been written, after close study of the manuscript, by Mr. Edward Ingle, a student of the colonial history of Virginia, and the author, when engaged in postgraduate work at the Johns Hopkins University, of a monograph, "Local Institutions of Virginia," later published as Nos. 2 and 3, Series 3, of the Johns Hopkins University Studies in Historical and Political Science;

Baltimore, 1885. His work upon the preface has been done merely because of his interest in the subject. I wish to express my hearty thanks to Mr. Ingle, not only for the actual performance of the task, but also for the admirable spirit shown by him in carrying it through.

H. R. McILWAINE.

PREFACE.

"Virginians of Affairs, 1757-1775" might be fit title of the collection of names printed on the following pages. The collection is interesting in its appeal to historian, antiquarian and genealogist as much because of the obscurity of the history of the manuscript colonial document upon which it is based and the uncertainty as to the purpose of the record itself as because of its value as an index of the personnel during the decade preceding the American Revolution of that influential body of men in the Old Dominion known as Justices of the County Courts.

The record has 106 paper pages, 15x10 inches, many of them beautifully watermarked. A number of the pages are quite fragile, and a few of them have been mutilated at their corners by time. They are protected by modern pasteboard covers, with leather back, encased in canvas. If they ever had an identifying title, it has been lost. The word, "Justices," and the figures, "1762 1775," stamped on the canvas case, and the inscription, "List of Justices 1762 1775," in lead-pencil on a flyleaf, all obviously of comparatively recent date, have suggestion in some of the notations in the record. But the dates are not as comprehensive as they should be. For, there are lists for 1757, 1760 and 1761, as well as for the years 1762-1775.

Coming to light in the Treasurer's office in the Capitol some years ago, the manuscript was moved, with other volumes in that office, to the State Library Building. Quite properly its original place would have been in the archives of the ancient colonial Council or of the Secretary of the Colony, at Williamsburg. Probably it was brought to Richmond when that city became the capital of the State during the Revolution, and may have been among the records saved from fire when the General Court Building was burned in 1865.

In the manuscript are represented, in 253 lists of names, sixty-one counties, the whole number existing in 1775. They were Accomac, Albemarle, Amelia, Amherst, Augusta, Bedford, Berkeley, Botetourt, Brunswick, Buckingham, Caroline, Charles City, Charlotte, Chesterfield, Culpeper, Cumberland, Dinwiddie, Dunmore (subsequently Shenandoah), Elizabeth City, Essex, Fairfax, Fauquier, Fincastle (subsequently Montgomery, Washington and Kentucky), Frederick, Goochland, Gloucester, Halifax, Hampshire, Hanover. Henrico, Isle of Wight, James City, King and Queen, King George, King William, Lancaster, Louisa, Loudoun, Lunenburg, Mecklenburg, Middlesex, Nansemond, New Kent, Norfolk, Northampton, Northumberland, Orange, Pittsylvania, Prince Edward, Prince George, Prince William, Princess Anne, Richmond, Southampton, Spotsylvania, Stafford, Surry, Sussex, Warwick, Westmoreland and York.

The 253 lists contain an aggregate of 4,957 names. Only two counties have but one list each. Four counties have eight lists each. The range in number of lists for other counties includes three counties having seven lists each and fourteen having four lists each. There are frequent repetitions of the names of the same individuals in lists in different years or at different times within the same year, in lists showing removal from one county to another and in lists reflecting the creation of new counties from parts of old ones, as, for instance, Botetourt from Augusta, and Fincastle from Botetourt. So, the 4,957 names actually represent approximately 2,000 individuals.

There is no unvarying chronological or alphabetical order in the arrangement of the lists. The first entry is headed "King William, April 11th, 1764." Across the page from it is "King George, November 22nd, 1762." On page 2 "Lancaster, July 30, 1762," is opposite "Louisa, December 21, 1764," and is followed by "Goochland, December 21, 1764." On page 4 "Albemarle, April 10, 1761," follows "Middlesex, June 12, 1765," and is followed on page 5 by "Nansemond, May 2, 1764." On page 6, "Northumberland, June 7, 1757," is followed by "Northumberland, April, 1762." Even where there are a number of counties carrying the same date, for example, November 6, 1766, no order in arrangement in the manuscript is apparent.

Entries were made at different times and by different hands. This variation is also marked in the notations upon the lists as a whole or upon individual names. Among the latter are, written out or abbreviated, such memoranda as "dead," "removed," "refuses," "to be left out," "refuses to qualify," "not in county," "resigned for five years," "removed out of the colony" and "out of colony."

In 250 of the lists the justices of the quorum are indicated. In seventy-three of the lists the sheriff is designated, and in seven of them the clerk.

Twenty-one of the lists have no comment indicating what use was made of them, seventy-five of them have notation that commission was issued, and one hundred and fifty-seven of them are marked only as having been examined. The record as to commission, in full or abbreviated, is "General Commission Issued" or "General Commission of Oyer and Terminer Issued," in one case, that for Loudoun County, June 15, 1768, the phrasing being "General Commission of Oyer and Terminer and Dedimus issued."

Seldom is there a notation, as that on the list for Orange county, April 12, 1768, showing that the commission had been issued on the date at the head of the list. The list for James City county, dated at its head, June 12, 1767, was marked, "Ex'd Reversed by the Governor." The list, repeated on the same page and as of July 8, 1767, was marked "Exam'd Genl Com^n Iss^d 12th Decr 1767."

---

[1]The manuscript is not folioed. Numbers used here are to identify pages.

The first record of a general commission issued is on the list for Lancaster county, dated July 30, 1762, and the last is on the list for Warwick county, dated October 25, 1770;

The list for Princess Anne county, dated November 24, 1762, has record of commission issued as of December 15, 1767, and the one for Fairfax county, dated December 7, 1764, has a record as of November 21, 1767.

Dunmore county, created from a part of Frederick county under an act of Assembly of 1772, and later becoming Shenandoah county, appears only twice in the manuscript. Its list for October 26, 1773, has the notation: "The Commission of the Peace for this miscarried, and must be sent to the Clerk when the Governor comes to Town."

Under the list for Accomac county, dated June 13, 1771, is the abbreviation "ch," for "charged." This notation as to charging appears thirty-five times, the last time on the list for Augusta county, April 20, 1775, the last entry in the manuscript.

Under the first list in the manuscript—that for King William county, dated April 11, 1764—are the words: "See at the other end for the Lists of Justices for 13 Counties."

There is nothing to suggest what is meant by "the other end." On the last eight pages of the volume are the lists for thirteen counties, one of the counties—Norfolk—having three lists, dated 1773, 1774 and 1775, respectively, and one county—Augusta—having two lists, dated 1774 and 1775, respectively. The last entries—those for Norfolk, Accomac and Augusta—are as of April 20, 1775. In the early morning of that day, Governor Dunmore had caused the powder to be removed secretly from the magazine at Williamsburg. Thenceforth he had no concern about commissioning justices in Virginia. If pages 98-105 are "the other end" mentioned on page 1, there is nothing in the list of the thirteen counties—Accomac, Augusta, Bedford, Botetourt, Brunswick, Buckingham, Dinwiddie, Essex, Lancaster, New Kent, Norfolk, Pittsylvania and Princess Anne, all as of 1774, with three repeated in 1775—indicating why they should have been chosen from among many others for special mention on the first page of the record.

It is possible that the mention may have referred to a list of counties of an earlier date than 1775, thus pointing toward the year when the record was begun. It may have been that that year was 1767. In the last two months of that year, a few weeks before the death of Lieutenant Governor Fauquier, commissions for twenty-nine counties were issued, twenty of them on December 15. Records of them are scattered over pages 5 to 31, inclusive, together with records of eight commissions issued, with no date given, seven issued in 1768, one issued in January, 1767, and forty-five lists with no

record of commission. The data of twenty-nine counties, including
the numbers of the pages upon which the lists of Justices appear,
the dates at the heads of the lists and the dates of the commissions,
follow:

County.	Page.	Head Date.	Commission Date.
Nansemond	5	May 7, 1765	December 11, 1767
Princess Anne	7	November 24, 1762	December 15, 1767
Fairfax	10	December 7, 1764	November 21, 1767
Chesterfield	15	November 6, 1766	November , 1767
King William	16	November 6, 1766	November 21, 1767
James City	17	July 8, 1767	December 12, 1767
New Kent	17	June	December 15, 1767
Hanover	18	July 23, 1767	December 15, 1767
Stafford	18	July 27, 1767	November 14, 1767
Amherst	20	November 24, 1766	December 15, 1767
Dinwiddie	20	November 24, 1766	November 27, 1767
Buckingham	22	March 25, 1767	December 15, 1767
Charles City	22	March 25, 1767	December 15, 1767
Bedford	23	April 3, 1767	December 15, 1767
Elizabeth City	23	April 3, 1767	December 15, 1767
York	24	April 3, 1767	December 15, 1767
Goochland	25	April , 1767	December 15, 1767
Culpeper	25	April 29, 1767	December 15, 1767
Pittsylvania	26	May 8, 1767	December 15, 1767
Halifax	27	October 22, 1767	December 15, 1767
Frederick	27	October 22, 1767	December 15, 1767
Richmond	28	October 23, 1767	December 15, 1767
Loudoun	28	October 23, 1767	December 15, 1767
Accomac	29	October 23, 1767	December 15, 1767
Middlesex	29	October 29, 1767	December 15, 1767
Hampshire	29	October 29, 1767	December 15, 1767
Northumberland	30	November 26, 1767	November 26, 1767
Caroline	30	December 11, 1767	December 11, 1767
Norfolk	31	December 11, 1767	December 14, 1767
Fairfax	31	December 11, 1767	December 15, 1767

Within the space of less than four weeks, two commissions were
issued for Fairfax county. The commissions for Northumberland
and Caroline counties were issued on the same dates as those carried at the head of the lists of Justices, a marked variation from
the usual procedure. The arrangement of the lists on pages 20-31
has a semblance of approach to chronological order. These facts
suggest that the compilation of the record may have been begun
in 1767, as Governor Fauquier issued, under a special act of 1765,
commissions of Oyer and Terminer to many justices, and that the

lists of earlier years were at that time recorded from existing memoranda.[2]

Such a compilation would have given the Governor a handy working basis for continuing Justices in their positions, for filling vacancies in their number caused by death, removal from a county or disinclination to serve, or for making entirely new appointments. The record, once begun, was probably carried on regularly until royal government in Virginia came to an end. The checking showing that the lists in the compilation had been examined may date from the provision of May, 1776, for continuance of administration of justice by "present Magistrates."[3]

The number of names in the 253 lists in the manuscript ranges from sixteen in Northumberland county, June 7, 1757; thirteen in Orange county, May 24, 1760, and sixteen in Albemarle county April 10, 1761, the lists bearing the earliest three dates, to seventeen in Accomac county, twenty-five in Norfolk county and forty-three in Augusta county, all of April 20, 1775, the last three entries. Standing in their respective communities of the men whose names appear in the lists may be fairly indicated in the following groups of four in each of the sixty-one counties of 1775, the selection being made more or less at random:

Accomac: Covington Corbin, Thomas Parramore, Thomas Teackle and Tully Robinson Wise.

Albemarle: Isaac Coles, Thomas Jefferson, Matthew Maury and Nicholas Meriwether.

Amelia: William Archer, William Crawley, Alexander Erskine and Charles Irby.

Amherst: William Cabell, James Dillard, John Rose and Zachariah Taliaferro.

Augusta: James Craig, William Crawford, Alexander McClanachan and James McDowell.

Bedford: Jeremiah Early, Samuel Hairston, Charles Lynch and Richard Stith.

Berkeley: John Neville, James Nourse, Thomas Rutherford and Thomas Swearingen.

Botetourt: Andrew Lewis, John Maxwell, David Robinson and Stephen Trigg.

Brunswick: Nicholas Edmunds, Sylvanus Stokes, James Wall and Douglas Wilkins.

Buckingham: John Cabell, William Cannon, John Johns and Thomas Patteson.

<hr>

[2] The watermark in some of the sheets may serve to solve the problem of the date of the compilation.
[3] Hening, IX, 126.

Caroline: John Armistead, Lunsford Lomax, Edmund Pendleton and Robert Taliaferro.

Charles City: John Jacob Coignan Dansie, Benjamin Harrison, David Minge and William Green Munford.

Charlotte: Thomas Bouldin, Paul Carrington, William Goode and Matthew Marrable.

Chesterfield: Archibald Cary, Robert Kennon, Richard Royall and Thomas Worsham.

Culpeper: Robert Green, Richard Pollard, John Slaughter and Robert Throckmorton.

Cumberland: Thomas Davenport, Littleberry Mosby, Thomas Turpin and John Woodson.

Dinwiddie: John Banister, Robert Bolling, John Jones and William Withers.

Dunmore: Abraham Bowman, Taverner Beale, Burr Harrison and Abraham Keller.

Elizabeth City: Wilson Miles Cary, David Curle, George Walker, Jr., and George Wythe.

Essex: Robert Beverley, Archibald Ritchie, Thomas Roane and William Woddrop.

Fairfax: Sampson Darrall, George Mason, William Payne and George Washington.

Fauquier: William Blackwell, Richard Chichester, Thomas Marshall and John Moffett.

Fincastle: Samuel Crockett, William Ingles, James McGavock and William Preston.

Frederick: Thomas, Lord Fairfax, Isaac Hite, Charles Mynn Thruston and James Wood.

Goochland: Thomas Bolling, Tarleton Fleming, Thomas Mann Randolph and Matthew Woodson.

Gloucester: George Booth, Lewis Burwell, Mann Page, Jr., and Charles Tomkies.

Halifax: William Hoskins, Radford Maxey, Edward Wade and Thomas Yuille.

Hampshire: James Claypoole, Jr., Enoch Tunis, Henry Vanmetre and George Wilson.

Hanover: Nathaniel West Dandridge, Peter Fontaine, John Meriwether and Anthony Winston.

Henrico: Richard Adams, Samuel Duval, Richard Randolph and Peter Winston.

Isle of Wight: James Allen Bridger, Daniel Herring, Thomas Pearce and George Purdie.

James City: Robert Carter Nicholas, William Norvell, John Randolph and John Tyler.

King George: Horatio Dade, Samuel Skinker, Anthony Strother and William Thornton.

King William: Carter Braxton, Philip Whitehead Claiborne, James Quarles and Francis West.

King and Queen: Thomas Coleman, John Tayloe Corbin, Robinson Daingerfield and Richard Tunstall.

Lancaster: Hugh Brent, John Chinn, John Fleet and James Selden.

Louisa: Thomas Poindexter, Nathaniel Pope, Thomas Ballard Smith and Waddy Thompson.

Loudoun: Josiah Clapham, Francis Lightfoot Lee, John McIlhaney and Nicholas Minor.

Lunenburg: Tscharner DeGrafenriedt, David Garland, Thomas Pettus and Thomas Tabb.

Mecklenburg: John Camp, Thomas Erskine, Robert Munford and Sir Peyton Skipwith.

Middlesex: James Montague, Charles Neilson, Christopher Robinson and Ralph Wormeley.

Nansemond: Samuel Cahoon, Jeremiah Godwin, Anthony Holliday and Willis Riddick.

New Kent: Burwell Bassett, Richard Chamberlayne, William Massie and Foster Webb.

Norfolk: Cornelius Calvert, Matthew Phripp, John Tatem and George Veal.

Northampton: Severn Eyre, John Robins, Littleton Savage and John Stringer.

Northumberland: Spencer Mottrom Ball, Kenner Cralle, William Eskridge and Thomas Gaskins.

Orange: Reuben Daniel, James Madison, Francis Moore and Richard Thomas.

Pittsylvania: Robert Chandler, Archibald Gordon, Hugh Innes and Benjamin Langford.

Prince Edward: Thomas Haskins, John Leigh, John Nash and Abraham Venable.

Prince George: Richard Bland, John Gilliam, Richard Kidder Meade and Peter Poythress.

Prince William: William Carr, Jesse Ewell, Howson Hooe and Foushee Tebbs.

Princess Anne: John Hancock, Richard Hack Moseley, William Nimmo, Jr., and Anthony Walke.

Richmond: William Brockenbrough, Landon Carter, Robert Wormeley Carter and Charles Fauntleroy.

Southampton: Thomas Blunt, James Day Ridley, Benjamin Ruffin, Jr., and Thomas Williamson.

Spotsylvania: Robert Chew, Edward Herndon, Fielding Lewis and Charles Yates.

Stafford: William Brent, Townshend Dade, Henry Fitzhugh and Samuel Selden.

Surry: Thomas Bailey, Hartwell Cocke, William Drew and John Watkins.

Sussex: Nicholas Massenburg, William Parham, Thomas Vaughan and Nathaniel Wyche.

Warwick: William Diggs, Edward Harwood, Robert Lucas and Benjamin Wills.

Westmoreland: William Berryman, Daniel McCarty, Richard Henry Lee and John Turberville.

York: Jaquelin Ambler, Thomas Nelson, Jr., Peyton Randolph and Anthony Robinson, Jr.

This tithe of the individuals whose names appear as of the period 1757-1775 is representative of the larger body of men who administered local justice in colonial Virginia from the time, in 1619, when quasi-military rule over less than 1,500 white persons, comparatively few of them beyond the purview of authorities at Jamestown, began to yield to civil establishment. Between that time and 1634, when the country was divided into eight shires—James City, Henrico, Charles City, Elizabeth City, Warwick River, Warrosquyoake, Charles River and Accomack[4]—commanders of plantations were succeeded, as judges, by commissioners of monthly courts and marshals by sheriffs.[5] Monthly courts became county courts in 1643,[6] and commissioners became Justices of the Peace in 1662.[7]

Appointment of Justices of the Peace lay with the Governor and Council in the early stages of county development.[8] During the interregnum of the Commonwealth there were reflections of political tendencies of the period in attempts to modify such practice. Under Acts of the General Assembly the variations between 1652 and 1658[9] included election of the officials by the House of Burgesses, appointment of them by the Governor and Council upon recommendation by those already in office, limitation of appointment to such persons as should be "desired by the court," with a proviso a year later, "and confirmed by the Assembly." Upon the restoration of royal government, appointment of the Justices of the Peace was again centered in the Governor where it remained.[10]

Apparently, the number of commissioners, or justices, for a county or corporation was determined at first by the pleasure of the appointing power or the ability to get men to serve. One of the earliest commissions, that of March 20, 1629, for Elizabeth City, was to eight men, including two captains and two lieutenants. In com-

[4]Hening, I, 224.
[5]Hening, I, 125, 132, 133.
[6]Hening, I, 273.
[7]Hening, II, 70.
[8]Hening, I, 125.
[9]Hening, I, 372, 376, 402, 480.
[10]Hening, II, 69.

missions issued three years later, the number ranged from five to
seven men. Within the next twenty-eight years there must have
been a great expansion in the number for other reasons than necessity to meet an increase and a scattering of the population. For,
two years after the return of Governor Berkeley to power, it was
deemed necessary to pass an act of Assembly containing the following:

> "Whereas, the great number of commissioners in each
> county hath rendered the place contemptible and raysed fac-
> tions among themselves rather than preserve the peace of the
> people, **Be itt enacted** that the commissioners in each county
> be restrained to the number of eight (of which the sherriffe
> to be one) being at present the eight first in each commission,
> unless some knowne defect or too neere relation to some
> other of the commission shall render them incapable **And be
> itt further enacted** that the sherriffes place shall after this
> yeare be conferred on the first in commission, and so devolve
> to every commissioner in course.''.

This act, re-enforced in 1662, does not seem to have restrained
Governor Berkeley. But presently, with an enlargement of the
borders of settled areas in the colony, necessity for means of con-
venient and prompt administration of justice became far more potent
than inclination to use appointment of Justices of the Peace to
strengthen the personal following of an executive in the enlargement of the body of Justices in the counties. Accordingly, among
the revisions of 1710 was an act, virtually repeated in 1748, fixing
the number of Justices in each county at eight or more persons, four
of whom, one of them being of the quorum, to be the court "accord-
ing to the ancient custom and usage heretofore in that behalf prac-
tised."[12]

.The numbers in the lists in the manuscript indicate that the alter-
native "or more" had been fully accepted. In lists of 1765, for instance, appear Augusta, with 37; Brunswick, 16; Dinwiddie, 16;
King and Queen, 20; Mecklenburg, 13, and Spotsylvania, 21. Under
date of November 6, 1766, are Albemarle, 20; Amelia, 23; Amherst,
15; Charlotte, 29; Chesterfield, 22; Elizabeth City, 16; King William,
17; Loudoun, 18; Middlesex, 16; Prince Edward, 18; Prince George,
17, and Stafford, 27.

Monthly courts, with commanders of plantations presiding and
with others commissioned by the Governor, were designed to meet
conditions in outlying settlements that could not in justice or convenience wait upon the quarter courts held by the Governor and

[11]Hening, II, 21.
[12]Hening, III, 504; V, 489.

Council at Jamestown. The jurisdiction of these monthly courts, as well as that of individual commissioners, was comparatively narrow. It dealt with fewer than 1,500 persons. With the creation of counties having definite boundaries, the change of name from commissioners to Justices of the Peace, an increase in the number of such officials and in the number of counties as increasing population in Tidewater and Piedmont sent its streams across the Appalachians to people territory stretching away to the Mississippi and the Ohio, the importance of the Justices of the Peace and of the County Courts expanded.

In the period to which the "Lists of Justices" refers, when the population of the colony was approaching 500,000, the County Court consisted of four or more of the Justices, one of whom had to be "of the quorum." The County Court had jurisdiction in all causes in the county cognizable at common law or chancery, except (1) those criminal causes wherein the judgment, upon conviction, should be for the loss of life or member, (2) the prosecution of causes to outlawry against person or persons, and (3) all causes involving less than 25 shillings sterling or 200 pounds of tobacco.[13]

The first two classes of exceptioned causes were for the General Court at Williamsburg. To that Court appeal could be taken from the County Court in other causes except in suits at common law or in chancery in which the debt or damage, exclusive of costs, should not exceed ten pounds in current money or 2,000 pounds of tobacco, unless the title or bounds of lands were in question.

The County Court listed tithables, laid the county levy, recorded land conveyances, bound out poor children to trades, and combined the functions of orphans, probate and claims courts. The chief functionary of the Court, the Sheriff, was one of the Justices of the Peace. It was provided that he was to be appointed by the Governor from among three Justices nominated by the Court, to serve for one year, except in some cases where a term of two years was allowable.[14]

At one time, exception was made to the rule of monthly sessions of the County Courts in the cases of Brunswick, Fairfax, Frederick, Lunenburg, Albemarle and Augusta counties, to meet certain local exigencies.[15]

The third class of exceptioned causes were determinable by a single Justice of the Peace. He also was empowered to keep the peace generally, by warrant or by hand, and he could cause a traitor, a felon, a pirate, a rioter, a breaker of the peace or other criminal offender to be arrested and brought before him, any other Justice, or the County Court.

[13]Hening, I, 313; III, 504-16; V, 489.
[14]Hening, II, 78; III, 246; V, 489.
[15]Hening, III, 504-16; V, 489.

The large number of memoranda of commissions of Oyer and Terminer issued in 1767, in the closing months of the Fauquier regime, marks an extension of the powers of the county Justices. That applied especially to the trial of slaves charged with capital crimes. Apprehension on that score had been reflected in Acts of Assembly of 1692, 1705 and 1723, and was such in 1748 that, "to detect and prevent secret plots and dangerous combinations of slaves, free negroes, mulattoes and Indians," an act was passed by the General Assembly authorizing the Governor to issue commissions of Oyer and Terminer to "such persons as he shall see fit," for the trial of such cases.[10] Seven years later Governor Dinwiddie reported to the Commissioners for Trade and Plantations that, for the punishment of slaves committing capital crimes, a commission of Oyer and Terminer was issued by the Governor directed to the Justices of the Peace in the county where the offense had been committed to try the offender without a jury and to award punishment. About the same time, Dinwiddie wrote to Colonel Charles Carter, "The Villany of the Negroes on any Emergency of Gov't is w't I always fear'd."[17]

The Stamp Act of 1765 had a prompt reaction in Virginia that may well have been described as an emergency in government. It may, therefore, be regarded as not a mere coincidence that in October of that year the General Assembly formally authorized and enlarged what had, in the exercise of the discretion of the Governor, become a practice. Preamble to an act amending the act of 1748 recited that much unnecessary trouble and expense had been caused in sending to the Governor from different parts of the Colony for commissions of Oyer and Terminer for the trial of each particular slave, "which commissions issue of course to the justices of the county." It was, therefore, enacted that the Governor be empowered to issue commissions of Oyer and Terminer directed to the justices of each county empowering them "to try, condemn and execute or otherwise punish or acquit" all slaves committing capital crimes in the county and, "where any commission for constituting justices of the peace shall thereafter issue, a general commission of Oyer and Terminer for the purposes aforesaid shall be sent therewith, and directed to the same persons."[18]

In the light of events of the time this legislation is explanation of the difference in months or in years between the dates heading many of the lists and those indicating the time of the issue of commissions of Oyer and Terminer in 1767, the first date, a memorandum of the usual commission, and the second date, a memorandum of action under the act of October, 1765.

[16]Hening, Vol. III, pp. 102, 209; Vol. IV, p. 127; Vol. VI, p. 104.
[17]Dinwiddie Papers, Vol. I, p. 284; Vol. II, p. 102.
[18]Hening, Vol. VIII, p. 138.

In 1662, attempt was made to establish periodical visitation of County Courts by the Governor and one member of the Council, or by two members of the Council designated by the Governor.[19] The experiment lasted but a few months. It was found to be too expensive.

Bodily presence in the County Courts and active participation in their proceedings by the Governor were not needed to emphasize the widely permeating influence of the central authority at Williamsburg in all parts of the colony through the County Courts and the individual Justices of the Peace. Indeed, such ramifying contact with the intimate concerns of the people was not limited to circumstances of the administration of justice. Many of the Justices of the Peace were also close to fellow-citizens by virtue of their positions as Vestrymen, who had duties touching the conduct of parishioners. Many of them, too, were to be found in the House of Burgesses, thus linking together local and general affairs.

One must read the scholarly study by Dr. Philip Alexander Bruce, "Institutional History of Virginia in the Seventeenth Century," to gain a comprehensive grasp of the province of the Justices of the Peace in the first eighty years of the evolution of county government in Virginia. In R. T. Barton's introduction to "Virginia Colonial Decisions" (Boston, 1909) is found a very satisfactory treatment of the whole subject of colonial Virginia Courts, and the same may be said of Oliver Perry Chitwood's "Justice in Colonial Virginia" (Nos. 7 and 8 of Series 23 of the Johns Hopkins University Studies in Historical and Political Science; Baltimore, 1905). For accurate knowledge of the history of the formation of the counties, one must consult the interesting and valuable product of research, "Virginia Counties; those Resulting from Virginia Legislation," by Morgan Poitiaux Robinson, State archivist, published as a bulletin of the State Library.

The manuscript known as "List of Justices" complements and is supplemented by such standard works by Virginians as William Meade's "Old Churches, Ministers and Families of Virginia," Lyon Gardiner Tyler's "Encyclopedia of Virginia Biography," and William G. and Mary Newton Stanard's "The Colonial Virginia Register."

Biographical details thus accessible will prove that, from the body of Justices of the Peace graduated carvers from the wilderness of civilized communities and great Commonwealths, creators of advanced forms of human government in a new land, eminent leaders in military matters affecting the whole human race, and in lay affairs of church and State, Presidents, Cabinet members, Senators and Representatives in the Congress, Governors, State lawmakers and lawgivers, and most efficient peacemakers in quiet, undramatic, but not the less telling, walks of life.

---

[19]Hening, II, 64.

Tendency of the office of Justice of the Peace to become, by custom only, hereditary was to some extent apparent. That was natural in a social constitution such as that which developed during a century and a half of land acquisition in colonial Virginia. Personal favoritism on the part of a Governor and appreciation of the opportunity in appointments to the office of Justice offered for bulwarking an administration at the colonial capital may have figured now and then in the situation. Politics and human nature of the seventeenth and eighteenth centuries were no whit different essentially from human nature and politics in the nineteenth and twentieth centuries.

Judging, however, by the 2,000 names in the following lists belonging to the years immediately preceding the American Revolution, the colonial Justices of the Peace fairly met the requirements of the act of Assembly of 1662, that they were to be "of the most able, honest and judicious persons of the county."[20]

Justices of the Peace, in positions of honor and service and not of emolument, represented the genuine **aristoi** of colonial Virginia.

EDWARD INGLE.

[20]Hening, II, 69.

JUSTICES OF THE PEACE OF COLONIAL VIRGINIA, 1757-1775.

[Page 1]

King William
April 11th 1764.

Francis West
James Quarles
Bernard Moore   refuse to qualify
Thomas Moore   the same
William Cowne
Harry Gaines
Thomas Chamberlayne
Richard Squire Taylor   Sher.
John Quarles
Philip Whitehead Claiborne   Quo^r
Carter Braxton
Roger Gregory
John West
William Langborne   dead
Owen Gwathmey   &
William Spiller   Gent.

See at the other end for the Lists
of Justices for 13 Counties.

King George
November 22nd 1762

Samuel Donne   dead
John Triplett   dead
Thomas Jett
Charles Carter   jun^r
George Washington   rem^d
Samuel Skinker
Joseph Murdock   dead
William Rowley
William Newton
William Robinson
Thomas Skinker   rem^d
Anthony Strother   jun^r Quo:
William Cunninghame
John Knox   rem^d
Arthur Morson
Horatio Dade
Austin Brokenbrough
William Champe
Thomas Hodge
John Champ   jun^r &
William Thornton   Gent

[Page 2]

Lancaster
July 30, 1762.

William Taylor   dead
Thos. Pinckard
Dale Carter
James Ball
Richard Selden   dead
George Heale
John Fleet
Charles Carter   Quo:
Wm. Dymer
Martin Shearman
Richard Mitchell
Rawleigh Shearman   She^r
Thomas Bertrand Griffin
Richard Edwards
John Chinn   Gent   &
Rawleigh Downman
     Genl. Com^s Iss^d

Louisa
21 Decr 1764.

Charles Barrett
John Carr
Thomas Johnson
Robert Anderson
John Pettus
William Johnson   shf.
Charles Smith
Thomas Ballard Smith
Nicholas Johnson
Nathl Pope
George Thompson   Quor:
James Overton
Samuel Ragland
Thomas Poindexter
Cleveare Duke
Rob. Armistead
Thos. Johnson   Junr

Goochland
Dec.r 21st, 1764

John Smith
John Payne
William Miller
Joseph Pollard
James Cole
George Payne
William Merewether   Sheriff
Thomas Maner [Mann] Randolph
Thomas Bolling   Quo.
John Bolling
Thomas Fleming
Tarlton Fleming
William Mitchell
Josias Payne   Junior
Thomas Randolph
Richard Fleming
Matthew Woodson   &
Joseph Woodson   Gent.

[Louisa—Continued]
James Meriwether
Richard Anderson
Waddy Thompson   &
Wm. Phillips.
   Genl. Coms Issd

[Page 3]

Lunenburgh
Dec. 21, 1764

Lyddal Bacon
David Stokes
Joseph Williams
David Claiborne
Thomas Tabb
David Garland   Quo
Abraham Maury
Henry Blagrave
Tscharner Degrafenriedt
John Jennings
Christopher Billups   &
Thomas Chambers   Gent:

Hanover
June 14th 1764

John Henry
Richard Johnson
John Snelson
Essex William Winston
William Taylor   decd
James Littlepage   decd
Nathl West Dandridge

Loudoun
Oct. 23, 1764

Francis Lightfoot Lee
Fielding Turner
James Hamilton
Oeneas Campbell
Nicholas Minor
Richard Coleman   dead
Charles Tyler
George West
Josiah Clapham   refuses to Qualify
Francis Peyton
John McIlhaney   Quo:
James Lane
Lee Massey   removed
Craven Peyton
John Moss   junr
Philip Nowland
William Carr Lane
Leven Powell
John Peake   refuses
John Pearce   &
John Minor   Gent.   refuses

[Hanover—Continued]

John Syme
John Boswell
Anthony Winston   Sheriff
Samuel Overton
Samuel Gist   Sh.
Henry Gilbert
John Meriwether   Quo:
Peter Fountain
Wm. Macon   junior
Meriwether Skelton
John Starke
Wm. Thompson
Nelson Berkley
Francis Smith
Charles Goodall   decd
Samuel Meredith
Charles Smith
Thomas Garland
John Webb   &
Wm. Morris   Gent.

Charles City

[Not dated]

John Minge
Benjamin Harrison
Littleberry Hardyman
Wm. Hardyman
John Jacob Coignan Dansie
Wm. Avrill   Quo:
Peter Royster
Wm. Edloe   Sheriff
George Minge
Philip Par Edmundson   &
Wm. Kennon   Gent.   Exd.

[Page 4]

Middlesex

June 12th 1765

Henry Thacker   dead
Christopher Robinson
John Robinson   Sheriff
Ralph Wormeley
Gawin Corbin
William Churchill   refuses
James Mills
Robert Daniel
Lewis Mountague
Charles Neilson   Quo:
John Berry   refuses
William Hackney   refuses
Ralph Wormeley   junior
Nathaniel Carpenter
Robert Spratt
Clement Nicholson
Christopher Robinson   junior
Maurice Smith   &
James Mountague   Gent.
    Ex^d

Norfolk

Apr. 11th 1764

John Hutchings
William Ivy
George Veal
James Webb
Robert Tucker   jun^r
William Aitchison   Sher.
Matthew Godfrey
John Tatem   Quor
John Hutchings   jun^r
Thomas Veal
Maximilian Calvert
Joseph Hutchings
John Portlock
Cornelius Calvert   &
Samuel Hopper   Gent

Albemarle
April 10th 1761

Robt. Lewis
Thomas Walker
William Harris
Henry Martin
Matthew Jordam
John Fry
David Mills   dec'd
Mosias Jones   Quo: Sheriff
Edward Carter
Arthur Hopkins
Robert Harris   dec'd
John Lewis
Nicholas Lewis
Guy Smith
Nicholas Meriwether   &
John Henderson   Junr Gent.
     Ex^d

Halifax
Dec. 21st, 1764

Thomas Dillard
Robert Wooding
John Gordon
Thomas Cobbs   Sheriff
James Roberts   junior
William Stoakes
Edward Booker
Hampton Wade   dec'd
Nathl Terry
John Bates
Arch. Gordon
Thomas Dillards   Junior   Quo:
Hugh Innes
George Watkins
Thomas Green
Theophilus Lacy
Wm. Hoskins
John Coleman
John Donelson
James Bates
Armist^d Wathington [Wattington]
Walter Coles   and
John Wilson   Gent.
     Ex^d

[Page 5]

Nansemond
May 2nd 1764

Mills Riddick   dead
Jonathan Godwin
Anthony Holliday
Josiah Riddick
Willis Riddick
Henning Temble
Thomas Godwin
William Moore   Quo.
Henry Riddick   Shf.
Staples Ivy
Jeremiah Godwin
Edward Wright
Benjamin Baker
William Shepherd &
Samuel Cohoon   Gent.

Northampton
14 Sept 1761

Littleton Eyre   1
John Kendall   dead
Edward Robins
John Wilkins   2
John Bowdoin   3
Azel Benthall
John Stratton   4
Michael Christian   5   Sh.
Severn Eyre   6   Quo:
John Harmanson   7
John Robins   8
Nathaniel Savage
Pruson Bowdoin
Patrick Harmanson
John Stringer   9
Thomas John Marshall   &
Arthur Robins   Gent   10
     Ex^d

Nansemond
7th of May 1765
Johnathan Godwin
Anthony Holliday
Josiah Riddick
Willis Riddick
Thomas Godwin
William Moore
Henry Riddick
Staples Ivy   Sherif
Jeremiah Godwin
Edward Wright   Quor
Benjamin Baker
William Shepherd
Samuel Cohoon
William Wilkinson
Thomas Sumner
John King
Thomas Fisher
Mills Riddick   &
James Wright   Gent.   Ex'd
   General Commⁿ of Oyer & Ter-
   miner issued 11th December 1767

Caroline
Dec. 21st
Edmund Pendleton
Robt Gilchrist
Anthony Thornton   Sheriff
Wm Tyler
James Jameson   dec'd
James Tyler
Benj. Robinson   dec'd
Robert Taliaferro   Junr
Wm. Parker
John Taylor   Quo
John Baynham
Gabriel Throckmorton
Lunsford Lomax   Junr
Wm. Buckner
Walker Taliaferro
James Miller
William Woodford   &
Thomas Lowry   Gent.
   Ex'd.

[Page 6]

New Kent
[not dated]
William Macon   dead
Richard Littlepage
Thruston James
Richard Adams
Edmund Bacon   dead
Burwell Bassett
Edward Pye Chamberlayne
George Webb
Lewis Webb   Sher.
Francis Foster   Quo :
William Richardson
Thomas Adams
Stephen Forneau Hoomes
John Armistead   refuses
Foster Webb
Edward Power
Wm Daingerfield
James Hockaday   &
Wm. Massie   Gent :
   Ex'd

Northumberland
June 7, 1757
Spencer Ball   dead
Samuel Blackwell   dead
John Foushee
George Ball
Baldwin Matthews Smith   dead
Griffin Fauntleroy   dead
Wm. Taite
Richard Hull   Quo :
Argall Taylor   dead
Thomas Gaskins
Newton Keene
Kendall Lee   not in the Comm.
John Eustace
Joseph McAdam
Thomas Edwards   Junr   &
Moses Champion   Gent :   dead
   Ex.

Accomack
October 19th, 1762

John Wise dec'd
Littleton Scarburgh Major
Thomas Parramore
Edmund Allen
Wm. Bagg
James Bule dec'd
Charles Stokeley dec'd
Covington Corbin Sheriff
Thomas Byley
Isaac Smith Quo:
Tully Robinson Wise
John Watts
Isaac Dunton
James Arbuckle
Wm. Selby
John Wise Jun[r]
Southy Simpson
Daniel Gore and
Henry Fletcher Gent.
    Ex'd

Northumberland
April '62

Spencer Ball Shr. dead
John Foushee
George Ball
William Taite dead
Richard Hull
Thomas Gaskins
Newton Keene
John Eustace Quor:
Joseph McAdam
Spencer Mottrom Ball
Rodham Kenner
Winder Kenner
Samuel Blackwell
Charles Fallen &
George Payne Gent.
    Exam[d]

[Page 7]

Orange
May 24th, 1760

Benjamin Cave dead
James Madison
Francis Moore
Thomas Jameson dead
William Bell
Rowland Thomas Sheriff
Richard Thomas Quor:
Elijah Morton
Rueben Daniel
Richard Barbour
Joseph Thomas Jun[r]
James Walker &
Zachariah Burnley
    Exam'd
        Genl. Comm. Iss'd

Princess Anne
Nov. 24, 1762

James Kempe
Nathaniel Newton dead
Edward Hack Moseley
Anthony Moseley resigned for
    five years
Anthony Walke Jun[r]
Nathaniel McClanahan dead
Tully Robinson
John Whitehurst
William Keeling
David McClanahan Quo:
John Ackiss
Mitchell Phillips
Anthony Lawson Sheriff 1767
George Logan
John Hancock
Thomas Reynolds Walker
Edward Cannon &
Edward Moseley Gent:
    Ex'd
        Genl. Comm. Iss'd 15th Dec. 1767

Amelia
May 2nd 1764

Abram Green
Thomas Tabb
Samuel Terry
Wm. Archer
Wood Jones
Henry Ward   Sheriff   dec'd
David Greenhill   Sheriff
John Winn
John Tabb
Alexander Erskine   Quo:
Richard Jones
Wm. Crawley
Edmund Booker
Benj. Ward
Henry Anderson
Charles Irby
John Booker
John Scott
Robt. Munford   and
Thomas Munford   Gent.
    Ex'd

Amherst
Jan. 17th 1763

Wm Cabbell   Junior
James Nevill
Daniel Burford
George Stovall   Junior
Cornelius Thomas
John Bose   Quo:
David Crawford
Francis Meriwether
James Dillard
Ambrose Lee   &
Zachariah Taliafero   Gent.
    Ex'd

[Page 8]

Prince George
Nov. 22nd 1764

Richard Bland
Theophilus Field
Anthony Penniston   dead
Benjamin Cocke
Peter Poythress
William Poythress
Richard Bland   Junior Sheriff
Alexander Morrison Quo:
William Starke
Theophilus Field   Junior
Nathaniel Raines
Sir Peyton Skipwith   Baro:
Peter Eppes
Theodorick Bland   Junior
Nathaniel Harrison Junior
John Poythress   Junior &
James Murray   Gent.
    Ex'd

Prince William
Jan. 19th 1764

Henry Lee
James Nisbett   Sheriff 1770
Cuthbert Harrison   dead
Henry Peyton
James Scott   Clk
Howson Hooe
John Baylis   dead
Allen Macrae   dead
Foushee Tebbs
William Tebbs
Thomas Lawson   Quor:
Lewis Renoe
William Carr
John Hooe
Lynaugh Helm
James Douglas   dead
Archibald Henderson   in Briton
Daniel Payne

Brunswick

June 13th 1760

Nicholas Edmunds
Drury Stith
John Clack
Edmund Goodrich
Littleberry Mosby
Thos. Twitty
James Hicks   Junior
Christopher Mason   Sheriff
Isaac Bowe Nalton
Wm Thornton   Quo:
Henry Edmunds
John Pettway
Lemuel Lanier
Wm. Clack
Thos. Stith
John Jones   &
Benj. Warren   Gent
  Ex'd

Warwick

[Not dated]

Henry Scasbrook
William Harwood
William Diggs
William Dudley
Banjamin Wills
Harwood Jones
John Jones   Quo:
Francis Jones   Sher.
William Langhorn
Francis Leigh
Servant Jones
Thomas Haynes
Robert Lucas
Hind Russell
James Donsing

[Prince William—Continued]

Thomas Blackburn
Matthew Whiting
Spence Grayson   &
George Skinker   Gent   dead
  Genl. Comm. Iss'd

Cumberland

Jan. 17th 1764

George Carrington
Thomas Turpin   Sheriff
Nicholas Davis
Wade Netherland
Creed Haskins
John Fleming
John Netherland
Thomas Tabb
Thomas Davenport   Quo
Thomas Prosser
Carter Henry Harrison
John Mayo
Wm. Smith
Richard James
Thomas Turpin   Junior
John Woodson   &
John Raines   Gent
  Ex'd

[Page 9]

York

Dec. 9th 1761

Peyton Randolph Esq.
Dudley Diggs   Junr
John Norton   removed
Armistead Lightfoot   dead
William Allen
Robert Shield
John Prentis
Wm. Waters   dead
Robert Smith
Edward Ambler   dead
John Blair   Junior
Thomas Nelson   Junior   Quo:
James Tarpley   dead
David Jameson
Anthony Robinson   Junior   Sher.
Thomas Chisman   dead
William Graves

Buckingham
7th May 1765

Samuel Jordan
David Pattison
John Cannon
Joseph Cabbell
William Johns
Robt Bolling
Benj. Howard
John Staples
John Fern
George Hooper   Quo
Jacob Lindsey
Francis Moseley
Jacob Cabell
Abraham Daniel
Jeremiah Whitney
Joseph Epperson
Charles Patterson
James Anderson   &
Joseph Benning   Gent.
  Ex'd

[York—Continued]
James Cocke
James Pride
Wm. Stevenson
Nicholas Dickson   dead
James Burwell   &
William Holt   Gent.   removed
  Ex'd

Gloucester
April 30th 1765

Robert Thochmorton
James Hubard
Warner Lewis
John Page
Francis Tomkies
Thos. Whiting
Lewis Burwell
Peter Beverly Whiting   Quo:
John Hughs
Thos. Smith
John Page   Junior
William Armistead
James Hubard   Junior
Kemp Whiting
George Booth   &
Charles Tomkies   Gent.
  Ex'd

[Page 10]

[part of page torn off]
[Fair]fax County
Dec. 7th 1764

[George] William Fairfax
[William] Ellzey
[John We]st
[George] Mason
[Dan]iel McCarty
[John] Carlyle
[Wil]liam Ramsay
[Ch]arles Broadwater
[Th]omas Colvill   dead
[Jo]hn West   Junior
[Br]yan Fairfax
[Sa]mpson Dorrell   Sher.
[Town]shend Dade   Quo:
[Hen]ry Gunnell

Amelia County
Dec' 18th 1764

Abraham Green
Thomas Tabb
Samuel Terry   dead
Wm. Archer
Wood Jones
Henry Ward   Sher.   dead
David Greenhill   Sher.
John Winn
John Tabb
Alexander Erskine
Richard Jones
Wm. Crawley
Edmund Booker   Quo:
Benjamin Ward
Henry Anderson   refuses

[Fairfax—Continued]
[M]armaduke Beckwith
Robert Adam
John Hunter   dead
Richard Sanford
Wm. Payne
Benjamin Grayson
William Adams
Edward Blackburn
Hector Ross   &
Alexander Henderson   Gent.
  Exam'd
    A General Comm. of Oyer &
  Terminer issued 21st Nov. 1767.

Culpeper
Oct. 20th 1762

Wm Green
Ambrose Powell
Thomas Scott
Nathl. Pendleton
Daniel Brown
Robert Green
Wm Williams
John Strother
Wm Brown
Joseph Wood   Quo:
John Slaughter
James Barbour   Junior
Henry Pendleton
Benj. Roberts
Wm. Kirtley
Wm Eastham
James Slaughter   Sher.
Henry Field   Junr.   &
Geo. Witherall   Gent.
  Ex'd

[Amelia—Continued]
Charles Irby   refuses
John Booker
John Scott
Robert Munford   &
Thomas Munford   Gent.
  Ex'd

Hanover
June 14th 1764

John Henry
Richard Johnson
John Snelson
Essex William Winston
Wm. Taylor   dead
James Littlepage   dead
Nathl. West Dandridge
John Sims
John Boswell
Anthony Winston
Samuel Overton
Samuel Gist
Henry Gilbert
John Meriwether   Quo.
Peter Fountain
Wm Macon   Junior
Meriwether Skelton
John Stàrke
William Thompson
Nelson Berkley
Francis Smith
Charles Goodall   dead
Saml. Meredith
Charles Smith
Thos Garland
John Webb   &
Wm. Morris   Gent.
  Ex'd

[Page 11]

Mecklenburg
Dec. 21, 1764

Robert Munford
Richard Witton
Samuel Tarry [Terry]   dead
John Speed

Charlotte
Dec. 21, 1764

Paul Carrington
Thomas Read
Thomas Boulden
Matthew Marrable

[**Mecklenburg**—Continued]
Henry Delony
Edmund Taylor
John Camp   Quo
Benjamin Baird
Thomas Erskin
John Potter
John Cox
Thomas Anderson
John Speed   Jr.
   Ex'd

Mecklenburg
March 1st 1765

Robert Munford
Richard Witton   Sher.
John Speed
Henry Deloney
Edmund Taylor
John Camp
Benjamin Baird   Quo:
Thomas Erskin
John Potter
John Cox
Thomas Anderson
John Speed   Junior   &
Samuel Hopkins   Gent:

[**Charlotte**—Continued]
James Hunt   Sheriff.
James Taylor
Thomas Bedford
Wm. Goode   Quo:
David Caldwell
Elisha White
Thomas Spencer
Joseph Moreton [Morton]
John White   &
Henry Isbell   Gent
   Ex'd

Brunswick
May 1st 1765

Nicholas Edmunds
Drury Stith
John Clack
Edward Goodrich
Christopher Mason   Sher.
Isaac Rowe Walton
William Thornton   Quor:
Thomas Stith
John Jones
James Wall
William Stith
Sterling Edmunds
Henry Cocke
Silvanus Stokes
Exum Williamson   &
Thomas Washington   Gent:

[Page 12]

Augusta
June 12th 1765

John Chiswell   dead
John Buchanan   dead
John Wilson
Silas Hart
Andrew Lewis   Shf.
James Lockart
Richard Wood
Robert Brakenridge
   [Breckenridge]
Patrick Martin
William Preston

King & Queen
June 12th 1765

John Robinson   Esq.   dead
Richard Tunstall
Henry Lyne
Philip Rootes   Sheriff
George Brook
Richard Shakleford
John Pendleton
Robert Brooking
John Richards
Thomas Read Rootes   Quo
John Ware

[Augusta—Continued]

John Bowyer
John Dickenson
John Christian
Daniel Smith
John Archer
Archibald Alexander
Israel Christian
Matthew Patton
John Maxwell   Quo:
John Poage
Felix Gilbert
Abraham Smith
James Trimble
Charles Lewis
Samuel McDowell
George Moffet
Benjamin Hawkins
Francis Berkley
Andrew Bird
Alexander Boyd   dead
David Robinson
William Fleming
Sampson Mathews
Alexander McClanahan
George Skillern
Benjamin Estell   &
William Bowyer   Gent
   Ex'd
   General Comm Issued

[King and Queen—Continued]

Clack Row
William Fleet
Armistead Bird
Tunstall Banks
Baylor Walker
William Lyne   &
Thomas Coleman   Gent:
   Ex'd

Elizabeth City
8th April 1762

George Wythe
Wilson Cary
Robert Armistead
Cary Selden
Wilson Miles Cary
George Walker
George Walker   Junior
David Curle   Quo:
George Wray   Sh:
John Tabb   Jr.
James Wallace
James Westwood
Walter McClurg
James Balfour
William Armistead   &
Joseph Selden   Gent:
   Ex'd

[Page 13]

Spotsylvania
July 2nd 1765

Larkin Chew
Benjamin Grymes
Feilding Lewis
Charles Dick
Beverly Winston   Sheriff
Joseph Brock
John Carter
Robert Goodloe
John Scandland Crane
William Smith
Roger Dixon.   Quor:
Thomas Wyatt

King & Queen
June 14th 176—(torn)

Richard Tunstall
Henry Lyne
Philip Rootes
George Brooke
John Pendleton   Sheriff
John Richards
John Whiting
John Ware
Clack Row   Quo:
William Fleet
Armistead Bird
Tunstall Banks

[Spotsylvania—Continued]
Charles Washington
Charles Yates
William Daingerfeild
John Stewart
John Roane
John Beverley Roy
Robert Chew
Zachary Lewis   &
Waller Lewis   Gent
  Ex'd Gen¹ Comm Issued.
New Commissions Iss⁴ 25 Ap¹ 1769

Dinwiddie
Aug. 16, 1765
William Broadnax
John Jones
Robt. Bolling
Robt Ruffin
Bolling Starke   Sh.
William Eaton
George Smith   Junior
Robt. Walker
William Watkins   Quo
Peter Jones
William Glascock
Herbert Haynes
Chas. Turnbull
Thos. Jones
William Withers
David Walker   &
Peter Jones   Junior   Gent:
  Ex'd

[King and Queen—Continued]
Baylor Walker
William Lyne
Thomas Coleman
Braxton Bird
Francis Gaines   &
William Todd   Gent:
  Ex'd

Dinwiddie
Aug. 1st 1763
Wm. Broadnax
John Jones
Robt. Bolling
Robert Ruffin
Bolling Starke   Sher.
Wm. Eaton
Robert Walker
Wm Watkins   Quo:
Peter Jones
William Glascock
Herbert Haynes
Charles Turnbull
Thos. Jones
William Withers
David Walker   &
Peter Jones   Junior   Gent:
  Ex'd

[Page 14]

Stafford
July 1st 1766
John Mercer
Thomas Ludwell Lee
Peter Daniel
Henry Fitzhugh
Francis Thornton
Thomas Fitzhugh
William Fitzhugh
John Stuart   Sher.
John Stith

Albemarle
Nov. 6th 1766
William Harris
Henry Martin
Matthew Jordan
John Fry
Mosias Jones
Arthur Hopkins   dead
Nicholas Lewis
Guy Smith   removed
Nicholas Meriwether

[Stafford—Continued]
John Washingon   Quor.   Sher.
Bailey Washington
Samuel Selden
Gowry Waugh
William Brent
William Bronaugh
  Ex'd
John Whiting
John Foster

King & Queen
July 2nd 1766

Richard Tunstall
Henry Lyne
Philip Rootes
George Brooke
Richard Shackleford
John Pendleton   Sherif
John Richards
John Whiting
John Ware
Clack Row   Quo:
William Fleet
Armistead Bird
Tunstall Banks
Baylor Walker
William Lyne
Thomas Coleman
Braxton Bird
Francis Gaines   &
William Todd   Gent:
  Ex'd
  Genl. Comm Issued

[Albemarle—Continued]
John Henderson   Jun'
Charles Lewis   Quor:
John Scott
William Burton
John Ware
Thos. Jefferson
John Walker
Charles Lewis Jr.
Robt. Lewis
Isaac Davis   &
David Rodes   Gent:
  Ex'd
  Genl. Comm. issd. Feb. 1768
Amelia
Nov. 6th 1766

Abraham Green
Thomas Tabb   dead
William Archer
Wood Jones
David Greenhill
John Winn
John Tabb
Alexander Erskine   dead
Richard Jones ——————
William Crawley   Sher
Edmund Booker
Benjamin Ward   Quor:
John Booker
John Scott
Robert Munford
Thomas Munford
Vivion Brooking
Thomas Williams
Crispan Shelton   removed to
  Pittsylva.
Lawrence Wells
Christopher Hudson
Christopher Ford   and
Stephen Cocke
  Exam^d Genl. Comm. Issued

[Page 15]

Middlesex
6th Nov. 1766

Christopher Robinson   dead
John Robinson
Ralph Wormeley
Gawin Corbin
James Mills   Sherif
Robert Daniel
Lewis Mountague
Charles Neilson   Quor:
Ralph Wormeley   Junr
Nathaniel Carpenter
Robert Spratt
Clement Nicholson   rem'd.
Christopher Robinson   Junr Ref^d
Maurice Smith
James Mountague   &
Philip Mountague   Gent:
     Exam'd
     See farther

Amherst
Nov 6th 1766

William Cabell   Junr
James Nevill
Daniel Burford
George Stoval   Junr
Cornelius Thomas
David Crawford
Francis Meriwether
James Dillard   Quor:
Zacharias Taliaferro
Henry Rose
Hugh Rose
Daniel Gaines
Ambrose Rucker
Charles Rodes   &
Alexander Reid   Junr   Gent:
     Exam'd

Charlotte
Nov 6th 1766

Paul Carrington
Thomas Read
Thomas Boulden
Matthew Marrable
James Hunt
James Taylor
Thomas Bedford
William Goode
David Caldwell
Elisha White
Thomas Spencer   Quor:
Joseph Morton
John White
Henry Isbell
Edward Mosby
James Venable
Josiah Morton
James Boulden
Richard Booker   &
William Price   Gent:
     Ex'd
     Genl. Comm. Issued the —
     Feb. 1768

Chesterfield
Nov. 6th 1766

Archibald Cary
Richard Royall
John Archer
Seth Ward
Edward Osborne   Junr
Robert Kennon
Claiborne Anderson
John Markham
John Hylton   Sherif
Abraham Sallee
John Archer   Junr   Quor:
William Walthall
Thomas Worsham
Edward Friend
Thomas Bolling
Seth Ward   Junr
Joseph Bass
Robert Goode

[**Chesterfield**—Continued]
George Robertson
Jacob Ashurst
David Holt   &
Francis Osborne   Gent:
  Exam'd
  General Com. of Oyer & Term'
  Nov. 1767

[Page 16]

King William
Nov. 6th 1766

Francis West
James Quarles
William Cowne } To be left out
Harry Gaines   dead
Thomas Chamberlayne
Richard Squire Taylor
John Quarles   Sherif
Philip Whitehead Claiborne
Carter Braxton   Quo:
Roger Gregory
John West
Owen Gwathmey
William Spiller
Ferdinando Leigh
John Hill
Robert Brooke   &
William Aylett   Gent:
  Ex'd
  General Commission of Oyer &
  Terminer issued 21st Nov' 1767

Loudoun
Nov. 6th 1766

Francis Lightfoot Lee
Fielding Turner
James Hamilton
Eneas Campbell
Nicholas Minor
George West
Charles Tyler   dead
Francis Peyton   Sh:
John McIlhaney   Quor:
James Lane
Craven Peyton

Elizabeth City
Nov. 6th 1766

George Wythe
Wilson Cary
Robert Armistead
Cary Selden
Wilson Miles Cary
George Walker
George Walker   Jun'
David Curle   Quor: dead
George Wray
John Tabb   Jun'   Sh.
James Wallace
James Westwood
Walter McClurg
James Balfour
William Armistead   &
Joseph Selden   Gent:
  Exam'd

Prince George
Nov. 6th 1766

Richard Bland
Theophilus Field
Anth° Penniston   dead
Benjamin Cocke
Peter Poythress
William Poythress   dead
Richard Bland   Jun'   Sher.
Alexander Morrison
William Starke   Quor:
Theophilus Field   Jun'
Nathaniel Raines
Sir Peyton Skipwith   Barr'
Peter Eppes
Theodorick Bland   Jun'

[**Loudoun**—Continued]
John Moss   Junr
Philip Noland
William Carr Lane
Leven Powell
John Pearce
William Douglas   &
Spence Grayson   Gentlemen
  Ex^d

[**Prince George**—Continued]
Nathaniel Harrison   Junr
John Poythress   Junr
James Murray   &
John Laforey   Gent: removed
  Exam'd
  Genl. Comⁿ Iss^d

[Page 17]

James City
June 12th 1767
John Randolph   Esqr
Richard Taliaferro
Lewis Burwell
Philip Johnson   Sh:
Thruston James
Edward Champion Travis
Robert Carter Nicholas
John Tyler
Edward Ambler
Dudley Richardson   Quo:
William Richardson
William Norvell
William Spratley
Edward Power
Benjamin Weldon
John Cooper
Charles Barham
Hudson Allen   &
Richardson Henley   Gent:
  Ex'd
  Reversed by the Governor.

New Kent
June [date torn]
Richard Littlepage   dead
Richard Adams
Burwell Bassett
Edward Pye Chamberlayne
George Webb
Lewis Webb
Francis Foster   Sh:
Julius King Burbidge
Wm. Marston
Thomas Adams   Quo:
Stephen Forneau Hoomes
Foster Webb
Wm. Daingerfield
John Hopkins
James Hockaday
Wm Massie
Peter Russell
Richard Chamberlayne   &
John Lewis   Gent:
  Ex'd
  Gen. Commⁿ Iss^d 15th Decr 1767

James City
July 8th 1767
John Randolph   Esqr
Richard Taliaferro
Lewis Burwell
Philip Johnson   Sh:
Thruston James
Edwd. Champion Travis
Robt. Carter Nicholas
John Tyler
Edward Ambler

[James City—Continued]
Dudley Richardson   Quo:
William Richardson
William Norvell
William Spratley
Edward Power
Benjamin Welden
John Cooper
Charles Barham
Hudson Allen   &
Richardson Henley
  Exam'd
  Gen¹ Comⁿ Issᵈ 12th Decʳ 1767

[Page 18]

Hanover
July 23d 1767 [Page torn]

[John] Henry
Richard Johnson
John Snelson
Essex William Winston
Nathaniel West Dandridge
John Syme
John Boswell
Anthony Winston   Sher:
Samuel Overton
Henry Gilbert
John Meriwether
William Macon   Junior   Quo:
Meriwether Skelton
John Starke
William Thompson
Nelson Berkley
Francis Smith
Samuel Meredith
Thomas Garland
John Webb
Garland Anderson
Charles Crenshaw   &
Geddes Winston   Gent:
  Ex'd
  Gen¹ Comⁿ Issᵈ 15th Decʳ 1767

Stafford
July 27th 1767

John Mercer   dead
Thomas Ludwell Lee
Peter Daniel
Henry Fitzhugh
Francis Thornton
Thomas Fitzhugh
William Fitzhugh
John Stuart   dead
John Stith   dead
John Washington   Sher:
Bailey Washington
Samuel Selden
Gowry Waugh
William Brent
William Bronaugh
Thomson Mason   removed
John Alexander   dead
Traverse Daniel   Quor:
Robert Washington
Lawrence Washington
Charles Stuart   dead
Samuel Washington   removed
William Fitzhugh Junʳ removed
John Brown
Wm. Ederington
William Adie   &
John James   Gent: Examᵈ
  General Comm: of Oyer &
  Termʳ issᵈ 14 Nov. 1767.

[Page 19]

Prince Edward
Novr 6th, 1766

John Nash
Abraham Venable
Joel Watkins
John Nash   Junr
Thomas Scott
Thomas Haskins
James Scott
Peter Legrand
John Leigh   Quor:
Henry Watkins
Peter Johnston
John Morton
Abner Nash
Charles Venable
Nathl Venable
Benjamin Haskins
William Booker   &
Philemon Holcombe   Gent.
   Exam^d
   Genl Comm^{an} Issued

Stafford
Novr 6th 1766.

John Mercer
Thomas Ludwell Lee
Peter Daniel
Henry Fitzhugh
Francis Thornton
Thomas Fizhugh
William Fitzhugh
John Stuart
John Stith
John Washington
Bailey Washington
Samuel Selden
Gowry Waugh
William Brent   Quor:
William Bronaugh
Thomson Mason
John Alexander
Traverse Daniel
Robert Washington
Richard Hooe

Sussex
Novr 14th 1766

John Mason
Nicholas Massenburg
Lawrence Gibbons
David Mason
Thomas Vaughan   Sher:
Michael Blow
Nathaniel Wych
Henry Gee
James Jones
John Cargill
John Mason   Junr
William Parham   Quor:
Richard Parker
John Walker
William Blunt
Ephraim Parham
Solomon Graves
Jesse Williamson
James Bell
George Booth
John Hunt   &
George Rieves   Gent:
   Exam^d
   Genl Com. Issued

Lunenburg
Nov. 24th 1766

Lyddal Bacon
Joseph Williams
Daniel Claiborne
Thomas Tabb
David Garland
Abraham Murry
Henry Blagrave
John Jennings
Christopher Billups
Thomas Chambers   Quor:
Thomas Winn
Richard Claiborne
William Gordon
John Ragsdale
Jonathan Pattason   Junr
Charles Hamlin

[Stafford—Continued]
Lawrence Washington
Charles Stuart
Samuel Washington
William Fitzhugh   Junr
Will: Ederington
Will: Adie
John James   Gent:
  Exam^d

[Lunenburg—Continued]
Jeremiah Glen   &
Everard Dowsing   Gent:
  Exam^d
    Gen. Com. of Oyer &c iss^d 30th
      of Jan 1768

[Page 20]

Amherst
Novr 24th 1766.

William Cabell   Junr
James Nevil
Daniel Burford   She:
George Stovall   Junr
Cornelius Thomas
John Rose
John Howard   moved   out   of
  the Col^y
Francis Meriwether
James Dillard
Zachariah Taliaferro   Quor:
Henry Rose   dead
Hugh Rose
Daniel Gaines
Ambrose Rucker
Charles Rodes
Alexander Reid   Junr &
Thomas Wiatt   Gent:
  Exam'd
Genl Com. iss^d 15th Decr 1767

Dinwiddie
Novr 24th 1766

William Broadnax
John Jones
Robert Bolling
Robert Ruffin
Bolling Starke
William Eaton
George Smith   Junr
Robert Walker
William Watkins
Peter Jones

Isle of Wight
Novr 24th 1766

James Bridger
Joseph Bridger
Dolphin Drew
Daniel Herring
Michael Eley
Nicholas Parker
John Eley   Junr
John Scasbrook Wills
George Purdie   Quo
Richard Hardy
Brewer Godwin
James Easson
William Davis
Thomas Peirce
Thomas Miller   &
John Lawrence   Gent:
  Exam^d
    Gen. Com. of Oyer iss^d 30th
      Jan. 1768

Brunswick
Novr 24th 1766

Nicholas Edmunds
Drury Stith
John Clack
Edward Goodrich
Christopher Mason
William Thornton
Thomas Stith   Sherif
John Jones
Sterling Edmunds
Sylvanus Stokes   Quor:
John Coleman

[**Dinwiddie**—Continued]
William Glascock
Herbert Haynes   Quor:
Charles Turnbull
Thomas Jones
William Withers
David Walker
Peter Jones   Jun[r]
Abraham Smith
James Greenway
James Walker
Edward Wyatt   &
Thomas Scott   Gentlemen
    Ex[d]
    Gen[l] Com[n] of Oyer & Ter-
        miner iss[d] 27th Nov[r] 1767
Another Comm. iss[d] 17th June 1768
                        [Page 21]

[**Brunswick**—Continued]
Thomas Simmons
James Wortham
William Edwards
Christopher Clinch
Thomas Peete
Douglas Wilkins
John Turner   &
Irvin Brown   Gent:
    Exam[d]
    Gen[l] Com. iss[d] 30th of Jan 1767

Mecklenburg
November 24th 1766

Robert Munford
Richard Witton
John Speed
Henry Delony
Edmund Taylor
John Camp
Benjamin Baird
Thomas Erskin
John Potter
John Cox   Quor:
Thomas Anderson
John Speed   Jun[r]
Samuel Hopkins
Robert Alexander
George Jefferson
Samuel Marshall
William Davis
David Christopher   &
Joshua Mabry   Gentlemen
    Exam[d]
    Gen Com. Iss[d] 29th Jan: 1768

Southampton
Dec[r] 4th 1766

Joseph Gray
Howell Edmunds   dead
Jesse Brown
Benjamin Simmons
Albridgton Jones
James Ridley
Peter Butts
Thomas Williamson
William Taylor
John Person   dead
Samuel Blow   dead
Nicholas Maget
Henry Taylor   Quo:
Charles Cosby
James Jones
John Wilkinson
Samuel Brown
Benjamin Jarrett   dead
William Person   dead
James Day Ridley
David Edmunds
Charles Briggs
Benjamin Clements   Jun[r]
Benjamin Ruffin   Jun[r]
Edwin Gray   &

King George
Nov. 24th 1766
John Triplett   dead
Thomas Jett
Charles Carter   rem^d
George Washington   removed
Samuel Skinker
Joseph Murdock   dead
William Rowley
William Newton
William Robinson
Thomas Skinker   removed
Anthony Strother   J^r
William Cunninghame   removed
John Knox   dead
Arthur Morson   Quor:
Horatio Dade
Austin Brokenbrough
William Champe
Thomas Hodge
John Champe
William Thornton
Thomas Landrum   clk
Dekar Thompson   dead
James Buchannon
Thomas Hord   Junr
Thomas Beny   and
John Triplett   J^r Gent:
   Exam^d
     Genl Com of Oyer &c iss^d 29th
     of Jan. 1768.

[Southampton—Continued]
Thomas Blunt   Gent:
   Exam^d
     Genl Com. of Oyer & Ter.
     iss^d 29th Jan 1768

Warwick
Decr 4th 1766
Henry Scasbrook
William Harwood
William Diggs
William Dudley
Benjamin Wills
Harwood Jones
John Jones
Francis Jones
William Langhorn   Sh:
Francis Leigh
Servant Jones
Thomas Haynes   Quo:
Robert Lucas
Hind Russell
James Dowsing
James Roscow   &
John Wills   Gent:
   Exam'd

[Page 22]

Henrico
Decemb^r 15th 1766.
Richard Randolph
Philip Mayo
William Lewis
John Ellis
Samuel Duvall
Bowler Cocke   Junr
Ryland Randolph
Isaac Younghusband
Joseph Lewis
Richard Adams   Quo:
Philip Watson

Buckingham
March 25th 1767
Samuel Jordan
Joseph Cabbell
Robert Bolling   Sherif
Benjamin Howard
John Fern
George Hooper
Jacob Lindsey
John Cabell   Quor:
Jeremiah Whitney
Charles Pattison
William Cannon

[Henrico—Continued]
William Smith
John Randolph
Thomas Watkins
Benjamin Duval
Daniel Price   Junr
George Cox
Nathaniel Wilkinson   &
Benjamin Johnson   Gent:
    Exam^d
        Gen Com iss^d the 29th of Jan.
        1768

New Kent
Dec. 15th 1766

Richard Littlepage
Thruston James   removed
Richard Adams
Burwell Bassett
Edward Pye Chamberlayne
George Webb
Lewis Webb
Francis Foster   Shr.
Wm. Richardson   removed
Thomas Adams   Quor:
Stephen Forneau Hoomes
Foster Webb
Edward Power   removed
Wm. Daingerfield
James Hockaday
William Massie
Peter Russell
Richard Chamberlayne   &
John Lewis   Gent:
    Exam^d

[Buckingham—Continued]
Charles May
John Johns
Samuel Taylor   &
William Anderson   Gent:
    Ex^d Genl Com. iss^d 15th Decr 1767

Charles City
March 25th 1767

another com. filled up with the
same names the 14th Sept. 1767.
John Minge
Benjamin Harrison
William Hardyman
Littlebury Hardyman   dead
John Jacob Coignan Dansie
William Acrill
Peter Royster   Quo   dead
William Edloe
George Minge
Philip Par Edmondson
William Kennon
Littlebury Cocke
William Green Munford   &
Edward Cocke   Gent: Ex^d
    Genl Com. iss^d 15th Decr 1767

[Page 23]

Bedford
April 3^d 1767

John Phelps
Robert Ewing
Charles Talbot
William Mead
Samuel Hairstone
Richard Stith
Joseph Rentiro
Jeremiah Early

Elizabeth City
Ap^l 3^d 1767.

George Wythe
Wilson Cary
Robert Armistead
Cary Selden
Wilson Miles Cary
George Walker
George Walker   Junr
George Wray

[Bedford—Continued]
Francis Callaway
William Trigg   Quor:
John Fitz Patrick
Thomas Watkins
Bowker Smith
Guy Smith
James Callaway
Charles Lynch
Hugh Challis
Francis Thorp
Joel Meador   &
John Pate   Gent.
   Exam^d
   Genl Com. issued 15th Decr 1767

[Elizabeth City—Continued]
John Tabb   Junr Sherif
James Wallace   quor:
James Westwood
Walter McClurg
James Balfour
William Armistead
Joseph Selden
Henry King
Gabriel Cay
James Mc Caw   &
Nicholas Curle   Gent:
   Exam^d
   Genl Com. iss^d 15th Decr 1767

[Page 24]

York County
Ap^l 3^d 1767

Peyton Randolph   Esqr
Dudley Digges   Junr
Armistead Lightfoot   dead
William Allen
Robert Shield
John Prentis
William Waters   dead
Robert Smith
Edward Ambler   dead
John Blair   Junr
Thomas Nelson   Junr
David Jameson
William Nelson   Junr quor:
Anthony Robinson   Junr Shf.
Thomas Chisman   dead
William Graves
James Cocke
Starkey Robinson
William Stevenson
Nicholas Dickson   dead
James Burwell
William Holt   removed
Jacquelin Ambler   Shf.
William Diggs   Junr
Augustine Moore   &
Lawrence Smith   Junr Gent.
   Exam^d
   Genl Com. iss^d 15th Decr 1767

Stafford
April 11th 1767

John Mercer
Thomas Ludwell Lee
Peter Daniel
Henry Fitzhugh
Francis Thornton
Thomas Fitzhugh
William Fitzhugh
John Stuart
John Stith
John Washington   Sher.
Bailey Washington
Samuel Selden
Gowry Waugh
William Brent   Quo
William Bronaugh
Thompson Mason
John Alexander
Traverse Daniel
Robert Washington
Richard Hooe   dead
Lawrence Washington
Charles Stuart
Samuel Washington
William Fitzhugh   Junr
John Brown
William Ederington
William Adie   &
John James   Gent:
   Ex^d

[Page 25]

Goochland April 1767	Culpeper April 29ᵗ 1767

<table>
<tr><td>

Goochland
April 1767

John Smith
William Miller
Joseph Pollard
George Payne
William Meriwether
Thomas Man Randolph
Thomas Bolling
John Bolling
Thomas Fleming
Tarlton Fleming　Quorum
William Michell
Thomas Randolph
Joseph Woodson
John Woodson
Joseph Royall Farrar
John Payne　Junʳ
Jesse Payne
William Harrison
Thomas Underwood
　Genˡ Comⁿ Issᵈ 15ᵗʰ Decʳ 1767

</td><td>

Culpeper
April 29ᵗ 1767

William Green　dead
Nathaniel Pendleton
Daniel Brown
Robert Green
William Williams
John Strother
William Brown
Joseph Wood
John Slaughter
James Barbour　Junʳ
Benjamin Roberts　Quorum
William Kirtley
James Slaughter
Henry Field　Junʳ
George Witherall
John Green
James Pendleton
Samuel Clayton
William Ball
Robert Throckmorton
Richard Pollard
Joseph Steward
　Exᵈ
　Genˡ Comⁿ Issᵈ Decʳ 15ᵗʰ 1767

Frederick
Apˡ 11ᵗʰ 1764

The Right Honᵇˡᵉ Thomas Lord
　Fairfax
Thomas Bryan Martin
Jacob Hite
John Hite
Isaac Hite
Van Swearingen
William Miller
Thomas Speak
John Greenfield
Thos. Rutherford
George Mercer
Adam Stephen　Quo.
Burr Harrison
Charles Smith
John Neavill

</td></tr>
</table>

[Frederick—Continued]
James Wood
Thomas Swearingen
Matthew Harrison
Angus McDonald
Daniel Sturges &
Thomas Waddlington   Gent:
    Exam[d]

[Page 26]

[Page torn]
[Hali]fax County
May 8th 1767
Robert Wooding
Thomas Cobbs
William Stokes
Edward Booker   dead
Nathaniel Terry
William Hoskins
James Bates
Armistead Wallington
Walter Cole
Thomas Yuille
John Lewis   Quo
William Thompson
Thomas Meriweather
John Foushee
John Williams
James Murdock   no Inhabitant
Nathaniel Baykdale [Barksdale]
Radford Maxey
John Orrill Tunstall
George Boyd
Ezekiel Slaughter   &
James Turner   Jun[r]
    Ex[d]

Pytsilvania [Pittsylvania] County
May 8th 1767
Thomas Dillard   Sen[r]   refuses
James Roberts   Jun[r]
Archibald Gordon
Thomas Dillard   Jun[r]
Hugh Innes
John Donelson
Theophilus Lacy
John Wilson
Peter Copeland
John Smith   Quo: refuses
John Dix
George Jefferson
Peter Perkins
John Vanbebber   removed
Haman Crity
John Hanby   dead
John Wembush
Robert Chandler   &
Benjamin Langford   Sherif
    Ex[d]
    Gen[l] Com[n] iss[d] 15th Dec[r] 1767

[Page 27]

Halifax
Oct[r] 22[d] 1767
Nathaniel Terry
Robert Wooding
Thomas Cobbs
W[m] Stokes
Wm Hoskins   Sh.
James Bates

Frederick
Oct: 23[d] 1767
The right hon[ble] Thomas Lord
    Fairfax
Thomas Bryan Martin
Jacob Hite
John Hite
Isaac Hite

[**Halifax**—Continued]
Armistead Wadlington
Walter Coles
Thomas Yuille
John Lewis   Quo:
Wm Thompson
Thomas Meriwether
John Foushee   dead
John Williams
Nathaniel Barksdale
Radford Maxey
John Orril Tunstall
George Boyd
Ezekiel Slaughter   &
James Turner   Gent
   Ex^d
      Genl Com^n iss^d 15th Decr 1767

[**Frederick**—Continued]
Van Swearingen
William Miller
Thomas Speak
John Greenfield
Thomas Rutherford
George Mercer
Adam Stephen
Burr Harrison   Quo:
Charles Smith
John Neavill
James Wood
Thomas Swaringen
Matthew Harrison
Angus McDonald
Daniel Sturges
Thomas Wadlington
The Revd Benj^a Sebastian
John McDonald   &
Taverner Beale   Gent:
   Exam^d
      Genl Com^n Iss^d 15th Decr 1767

[Page 28]

Richmond
Octr 23^d 1767
John Woodbridge
Landon Carter
John Smith
William Brockenbrough
Travers Tarpley   dead
John Tarpley
Wm Peachy
Robert Downman   dead
John Belfield
Robert Wormeley Carter   Quo:
John Plummer   Sh:
Thomas Beale
John Gordon
LeRoy Griffin
Thomas Glascock
Williamson Ball
Wm Ford
Wm Fountleroy   Junr   &
Robert Tomlin   Gent:
   Ex^d
      Genl Com^n iss^d 15th Decr 1767

Loudoun
Octr 23^d 1767
Francis Lightfoot Lee
Fielding Turner
James Hamilton
Oneas Campbell
Nicholas Minor
Josias Clapham
George West
Francis Peyton
John Mcilhaney
James Lane   Quor:
Lee Massey
Craven Peyton
John Moss   Junr
Philip Noland
Wm Carr Lane
Leven Powell
John Minor
Wm Douglas   &
Thomas Lewis   Gent:
   Ex^d
      Genl Com^n iss^d 15th Decr 1767

[Page 29]

Accomack County
Octr 23^d 1767
Littleton Scarburgh Major
Thomas Parramore
Edmund Allen
William Bagg
Covington Corbin
Thomas Ryley
Isaac Smith   Sher:
Tulley Robinson Wise
John Watts
Isaac Dunton   Quor:
James Arbuckle
William Selby
John Wise
Southy Simpson
Daniel Gore
Henry Fletcher
William Williams
John Smith
Thomas Teackle   Junr   &
George Stewart   Gent:
    Ex^d
       Genl Com. iss^d Decr 15th 1767

Warwick
October 29th 1767
Henry Scasbrook
Wm Harwood
William Digges
William Dudley
Benjamin Wills
Harwood Jones
John Jones
Francis Jones
[William] Langhorn   Sher:
[Francis] Leigh
    [Several names are torn off]

Middlesex
Octr 29 1767
Christopher Robinson   dead
Gawin Corbin
James Mills
Edmund Berkley
Robert Daniel
Lewis Mountague
Charles Neilson
Nathl Carpenter
Philip Grymes   Quo:
Robert Spratt
Maurice Smith
James Mountague
Philip Mountague
George Daniel
Thomas Kemp   &
Wm Roane . Gent:
    Ex^d
       Genl Com^n iss^d Decr 15th 1767

Hampshire
Octr 29th 1767
Thomas Bryan Martin
Henry Vanmeter
Solomon Hedge
Abraham Hite
Garrett Vanmeter
Jonathan Cooburn
Michael Stump
Felix Seymore
Thomas Parsons
Jonathan Heath
Isaac Eley   Quo:
Robert Parker
Abraham Johnston
Enoch Innis
Stephen Ruddell
James Seaton
George Wilson
John Forman
Simon Taylor
William McCracken.   &
Job Welton   Gent:
    Ex^d
       Genl Com^n iss^d 15 Decr 1767

[Page 30]

Northumberland
Novr 26th 1767

George Ball
Richard Hull
Thomas Gaskins
Newton Keene
John Eustace
Joseph McAdam
Spencer Mottrom Ball
Rodham Kenner
Winder Kenner   Quo:
Samuel Blackwell
Charles Fallen
George Payne
David Ball   Junr
Charles Bell
John Smith   Junr
William Ball
John Williams   &
Lindsey Opie   Gent.
 Ex^d
  Genl Com. of Oyer & Term^r
  iss^d the above day

Caroline
11th Decr 1767

Edmund Pendleton
Robert Gilchrist
Anthony Thornton
William Tyler
James Taylor
Robert Taliaferro   Junr
William Parker
John Taylor
John Baynham
Gabriel Throckmorton
Lunsford Lomax   Junr
Wm Buckner   Quo:
Walker Taliaferro
James Miller
Wm Woodford
John Buckner
Thomas Lowry
George Taylor
John Armistead
Wm Buckner   Junr
Samuel Hawes
Thomas Slaughter   &
William Jones   Gent:
 Ex^d
  G^l Com. of Oyer iss^d this 11th
  Decr 1767

[Page 31]

Norfolk
11th Decr 1767

John Hutchings   dead
Wm Ivy
George Veal
James Webb
Robert Tucker   Junr
·William Aitchison
Matthew Godfrey
John Tatem
John Hutchings   Junr
Thomas Veal
Maximilian Calvert   Quo:
Joseph Hutchings

Fairfax
11th Decr 1767

George William Fairfax
Lewis Ellzey
John West
George Mason
Daniel McCarty
John Carlyle
Wm Ramsay
Charles Broadwater
John West   Junr
Bryan Fairfax
Sampson Dorrell   Quo:
Townshend Dade

[Norfolk—Continued]
John Portlock
Cornelius Calvert
Samuel Hopper
Goodrich Boush
Malichi Wilson   Junr
Matthew Thripp
David Porter
Thomas Newton   Junr
John Wilson   &
John Taylor   Senr Gent:
   Ex^d
A General Com^n iss^d Decr 14th 1767

[Fairfax—Continued]
Henry Gunnell
Marmaduke Beckwith
Robert Adam
Richard Sanford
Wm Payne
Benjamin Grayson
Wm Adams
Edward Blackburn
Hector Ross
Alexander Henderson
George Washington   &
Daniel French   Gent:
   Ex^d
      Genl Com^n iss^d 15th Decr 1767

[Page 32]

Orange
April 12th 1768

James Madison
Francis Moore
William Bell
Rowland Jones
Richard Thomas
Reuben Daniel
Richard Barbour
James Walker   Quo:
Zachariah Burnley
Thomas Bell
William Moore
Lawrence Taliaferro
Andrew Shepherd
Thomas Barbour
Johnny Scott   &
William Pannell
   Ex^d
      Genl Com. of Oyer & Ter-
      miner issued the above day

Northampton
Ap^l 20th 1768

Littleton Eyre   dead
John Wilkins
John Bowdoin
John Stratton
Michael Christian

Goochland
May 7th 1768

John Smith
William Miller
Joseph Pollard
George Payne
William Meriwether
Thomas Man Randolph
Thomas Bolling
John Bolling
Thomas Fleming
Tarlton Fleming   Quor:
William Mitchell
Thomas Randolph
Joseph Woodson
John Woodson
Joseph Royall Farrar
John Payne   Junr
Jesse Payne
William Harrison
Thomas Underwood   &
Josias Payne   Junr Gent:

[**Northampton**—Continued]
Severn Eyre
John Harmanson
John Robins
John Stringer   Quo:
Arthur Robins
Thomas Dalby
John Respess
John Wilkins   of old Plantation
Littleton Savage
John Robins   Junr
Joachim Michael
William Christian   &
Henry Guy   Gent:
    Ex^d

[Page 33]

King & Queen
May 7th 1768

Richard Tunstall
Henry Lyne
Philip Rootes
George Brooke
John Pendleton
John Ware
Clack Row
William Fleet
Armistead Bird   Quor:
Tunstall Banks
Baylor Walker
William Lyne
Thomas Coleman
William Todd
Lyne Shackelford
Richard Tunstall   Junr
William Taliaferro   and
Gregory Smith   Gent:
    Exam^d

Stafford
May 26th 1768

John Mercer   dead
Thomas Lud: Lee
Peter Daniell
Henry Fitzhugh
Francis Thornton
Thomas Fitzhugh
William Fitzhugh
John Stuart
John Stith
John Washington
Bailey Washington
Samuel Selden
Gowry Waugh
William Brent
William Bronough
Thomson Mason
John Alexander
Traverse Daniel   Quor:
Robert Washington
Lawrence Washington
Charles Stuart
Samuel Washington
William Fitzhugh   Junr
John Brown
William Edrington
John James
William Adie
Yelverton Peyton

[Stafford—Continued]
Gerrard Hooe
Charles Alexander
Andrew Grant
John Gibson
John Chambers
Townshend Dade
William Hooe &
John Bronaugh Gent:
   Exam^d
      General Com^n of Oyer iss^d
      26 May 68

[Page 34]

Loudoun
June 15th 1768

Francis Lightfoot Lee
James Hamilton
Nicholas Minor
Josias Clapham
George West
Francis Peyton
John McElhaney
James Lane
Craven Peyton
Philip Noland
William Carr Lane   Quorum
Leven Powell
John Minor
William Douglass
Thomas Lewis
Simon Triplett
Stephen Donaldson
William Smith
George Sumners
Fleming Patterson &
Elijah Chinn   Gent   dead
  Ex^d
    Genl Com^n of Oyer & Term^r
    and Dedimus issued the 15th
    June 1768

Charlotte
June 16th 1768

Paul Carrington
Clement Read
Thomas Read
Thomas Boulden
Matthew Marrable
James Hunt
James Taylor
Thomas Bedford
William Goode
David Caldwell
Elisha White
Thomas Spencer
Joseph Morton   Quorum
John White
Henry Isbell
Edward Mosley
James Venable
Josiah Morton
James Boulden
Richard Booker
William Price
James Watkins
Thomas Carter
Joseph Moore
William Morton
Stephen Bedford   and
John Fuqua   Gent.

[Page 35]

James City
June 15th 1768
John Randolph   Esqr
Richard Taliaferro
Lewis Burwell
Philip Johnson
Edward Champion Travis
Robert Carter Nicholas
John Tyler
Dudley Richardson
William Norvell   Quorum
William Spratley
Benjamin Weldon
Richard Taliaferro   Junr
John Cooper
Charles Barham
Hudson Allen
Holdenby Dixon
Turner Henley   &
Joseph Eggleston   Gent.
   Examd
     A General Comn of Oyer &
      Termr issd

Fairfax
July 29th 1768
George W Fairfax
Lewis Ellzey
John West
George Mason
Daniel McCarty
John Carlyle
Wm Ramsey
Charles Broadwater
John West   Junior
Bryan Fairfax
Sampson Darrel
Townshend Dade   Quorum
Henry Gunnell
Marmaduke Beckwith
Robert Adam
Richard Sanford
Wm Payne
Benjamin Grayson   dead
Wm Adams
Hector Ross
Alexander Henderson
George Washington
Daniel French   &
Edward Payne   Gent:
   Examd
     General Commn of Oyer &
      Termr Issued

[Page 36]

Essex
September 8th 1768
William Daingerfield
Francis Waring
Simon Miller
Archibald Ritchie
Thomas Roane
William Mountague
John Upshaw
Samuel Peachy
Paul Micou
Charles Mortimer
Robert Beverly   Quor:
Meriwether Smith

Nansemond
Octr 19th 1768
Jonathan Godwin
Anthony Holliday
Josiah Riddick
Willis Riddick
Thomas Godwin
William Moore
Henry Riddick
Staples Ivy
Jeremiah Godwin
Edward Wright
Benjamin Baker
William Shepherd   Quor:

[Essex—Continued]
James Roy
John Corrie
Muscoe Garnett
Thomas Bowler
James Webb   Jun[r]
John Richards
Henry Garnett   &
Griffing Boughan
  General Commission Issued

[Nansemond—Continued]
Samuel Cohoon
William Wilkinson
Thomas Sumner
John King
Thomas Fisher
Mills Riddick
James Wright
David Meade
John Drew   &
Miles King
  Ex[d]

[Page 37].

Middlesex
Nov[r] 1st 1768
Ralph Wormeley
Gawin Corbin
James Mills
Edmund Berkley
Robert Daniel
Lewis Montague
Charles Neilson
Ralph Wormeley   Junior
Nathaniel Carpenter
Philip Grymes   Quor:
Robert Spratt
Maurice Smith
James Montague
Philip Montague
Augustine Smith
George Daniel   &
William Roane   Gent.
  Ex[d]
Gen[l] Com. of Oyer & Term. iss[d]

Albemarle
Novem[r] 1st 1768
William Harris
Henry Martin
Matthew Jordan
Mosias Jones
Nicholas Lewis
Nicholas Meriwether
John Henderson   Jun[r]
Charles Lewis
John Scott
William Burton   Quor:
John Ware
Thomas Jefferson
John Walker
Cha[s] Lewis   Jun[r]
Isaac Davis
David Rodes
Edward Carter
Isaac Coles   &
Roger Thompson   Gent.
  Ex[d]
  Gen: Com: of Oyer & Term:
  iss[d]

[Page 38]

Isle of Wight
Nov[r] 4th 1768
James Bridger
Joseph Bridger   dead
Dolphin Drew
Daniel Herring
Michael Ealey   Sherif

Cumberland
Nov[r] 4th 1768
George Carrington
Thomas Turpin
John Netherland
Thomas Tabb
Thomas Davenport

[Isle of Wight—Continued]
Nicholas Parker
John Eley   Jun[r]
John Scasbrook Wills
George Purdie
Nathaniel Burwell   Quor:
Richard Hardy
Brewer Godwin
James Eason   dead
William Davis   refuses
Thomas Pierce
Thomas Miller   &
John Lawrence   Gent.
    Exam[d]
        Gen[l] Com. of Oyer & Term:
        iss[d]

[Cumberland—Continued]
Littlebury Mosby
Carter Henry Harrison
John Mayo
William Smith   Quor:
Richard James
Thomas Turpin   Jun[r]
John Woodson
John Raine
Jacob Michaux
Joseph Carrington
Joseph Calland
Robert Smith   &
Edward Haskins   Gent.
    Ex[d]
        Gen[l] Com. of Oyer & Term:
        iss[d]

[Page 39]

Nansemond
Dec[l] 16th 1768

Jonathan Godwin
Anthony Holliday
Josiah Riddick
Willis Riddick
Thomas Godwin
William Moore
Henry Riddick
Staples Ivy
Jeremiah Godwin
Edward Wright
Benjamin Baker
William Shepherd   Quorum
Samuel Cohoon
William Wilkinson
Thomas Sumner
John King
Thomas Fisher
Mills Riddick
James Wright
David Meade
John Drew   &
Miles King
    Exam[d]
        Gen[l] Com. of Oy: & Term. iss[d]

Northampton
Dec[r] 22[d] 176[8]

John Wilkins
John Bowdoin
John Stratton
Michael Christian
Severn Eyre
John Harmonson
John Robins
Nathaniel Lytt: Savage
John Stringer   Quor:
Arthur Robins
Thomas Dalby
John Respess
John Wilkins   of old Plantation
Littleton Savage
John Robins   Jun[r]
Joachim Michael
William Christian   &
Henry Guy
    Exam[d]

[Page 40]

Isle of Wight
January 13th 1769
James Bridger
Joseph Bridger   dead
Dolphin Drew
Daniel Herring
Michael Ealey
Nicholas Parker
John Ealey   Junr
John Scasbrook Wills
George Purdie
Nathaniel Burwell   Quor:
Richard Hardy·
Brewer Godwin
Thomas Pierce
Thomas Miller
John Lawrence
Thomas Day   &
Timothy Tynes   Gent.
  Examd
   Gen: Com: Oyer & Term: issd

King & Queen
Febr 27th 1769
Richard Tunstall
Henry Lyne
Philip Rootes
George Brooke
John Pendleton
John Ware
Clack Row
William Fleet
Armistead Bird   Quor:
Tunstall Banks
Baylor Walker
William Lyne
Thomas Coleman
William Todd
Lyne Shakleford
Richard Tunstall   Junr
William Taliaferro   and
Gregory Smith   Gent.
  Examd
   Gen: Com: Oyer and Term:
   issd

[Page 41]

Gloucester
April 28th 1769
James Hubbard
Francis Tomkies
Thomas Whitinge
Lewis Burwell
John Hughes
Thomas Smith
John Page   Junr
Wm Armistead
Mann Page   Junr   Quo
James Hubbard   Junr
Kemp Whiting
George Booth
Charles Tomkies
William Hayes   dead
Warner Lewis   Junr
John Cooke   Junr
Francis Willis   Junr   &
George Booth   Jr   Gent
  Examd

Spotsylvania
April 25th 1769
Larkin Chew
Benjamin Grymes
Fielding Lewis
Charles Dick   ·
Beverley Winslow
Joseph Brock
John Carter
Robert Goodloe
John Scanland Crane
William Smith
Roger Dixon   Quo.
Thomas Wyatt
Charles Washington
Charles Yates
William Daingerfield
John Stewart
John Roane
John Beverley Roy
Robert Chew
Zachary Lewis   &
Waller Lewis   Gent
  Examd

[Page 42]

Chesterfield	Frederick
May the 3ᵈ 1769	May 10ᵗʰ 1769

Chesterfield
May the 3ᵈ 1769
Archibald Cary
Richard Royall
John Archer
Seth Ward
Robert Kennon
John Hylton
Abraham Sallee
John Archer   Junʳ
Thomas Worsham
Thomas Bolling   Quor:
Seth Ward   Junʳ
Joseph Bass
Robert Goode
George Robertson
Jacob Ashurst
David Holt
Christopher Branch
Branch Tanner
Benjamin Branch   &
Bernard Markam   Gent
   Gen: Com: &c issᵈ
     Exᵈ

Frederick
May 10ᵗʰ 1769
The Right Hon: Thomas Lord
   Fairfax
Thomas Bryan Martin
Ralph Wormeley   Senʳ
Jacob Hite
John Hite
Isaac Hite
Charles Dick
Van Swearingen
Thomas Speak
Thomas Rutherford
George Mercer
Adam Stephen   Quor:
Burr Harrison
Charles Smith
James Wood
Thomas Swearingen
Matthew Harrison
Angus McDonald
Charles Mynn Thruston
Samuel Washington
Taverner Beale
Warner Washington   &
William Miller   Junʳ   Gent.
   Examᵈ
     Gen: Com: issᵈ

[Page 43]

Chesterfield
May 10ᵗʰ 1769
Archibald Cary
Richard Royall
John Archer
Seth Ward
Robert Kennon
John Hylton
Abraham Sallee
John Archer   Junʳ
Thomas Worsham
Thomas Bolling
Seth Ward   Junʳ   Quor
Joseph Bass

Prince George
June 17ᵗʰ 1769
Richard Bland
Samuel Gordon
Peter Poythress
Alexander Morrison
William Starke
Theophilus Field   Junʳ
Nathaniel Raines
Sir Peyton Skipwith Bart:
Peter Eppes
Nathaniel Harrison   Junʳ   Quor:
John Poythress   Junʳ
James Murray

[Chesterfield—Continued]
Robert Goode
George Robertson
Jacob Ashurst
David Holt
Christoher Branch
Branch Tanner
Benjamin Branch
Bernard Markham   &
John Bott   Gent.
  Exam^d
    Genl. Com. iss^d

[Prince George—Continued]
Benjamin Harrison   Junr
Patrick Ramsay
John Gilliam   Junr
Richard Kidder Mead
Peter Randolph Bland
Edmund Ruffin   Junr
Thomas Harris   &
Hubbard Wyatt   Gent.
  Ex^d
    General Comm. iss^d

[Page 44]

Spottsylvania
June 19th 1769
Larkin Chew
Fielding Lewis
Charles Dick
Beverly Winslow
Joseph Brock
John Carter
Robert Goodloe
John Scandland Crane
William Smith
Roger Dixon   Quor:
Thomas Wyatt
Charles Washington
Charles Yates
William Daingerfield
John Stewart
John Roane
Robert Chew
Zachary Lewis   &
Waller Lewis   Gent:
  Examined
    General Com: &c

Chesterfield
June 20th 1769
Archibald Cary
Richard Royall
John Archer
Seth Ward
Robert Kennon
John Hylton
Abraham Sallee
John Archer   Junr
Thomas Worsham
Thomas Bolling
Seth Ward   Junr
Joseph Bass   Quorum
Robert Goode
George Robertson
Jacob Ashurst
David Holt
Christopher Branch
Branch Tanner
Benjamin Branch
Bernard Markham
Francis Eppes
John Botte   &
Francis Goode   Gent
  Ex^d
    General Comm: &c iss^d

[Page 45]

King & Queen
June 20ᵗʰ 1769

Richard Tunstall
Philip Rootes
George Brooke
John Ware
Clack Rowe
William Fleet
Armistead Bird
Tunstall Banks
Baylor Walker
William Lyne   Quor.
Thomas Coleman
William Todd
James Dickie
Robinson Daingerfield
Lyne Shackleford
Richard Tunstall .   Junʳ
William Taliaferro
Gregory Smith   &
John Tayloe Corbin   Gent.
    Exᵈ
    General Com. issᵈ

Stafford
July 18ᵗʰ 1769

Thomas Ludwell Lee
Peter Daniel
Henry Fitzhugh
Francis Thornton
Thomas Fitzhugh
William Fitzhugh
John Stewart
John Stith
John Washington
Bailey Washington
Samuel Selden
Gowry Waugh
William Brent
William Bronaugh
Thomson· Mason
John Alexander
Traverse Daniel   Quor.
Robert Washington
Lawrence Washington
Charles Steuart
Samuel Washington
William Fitzhugh   Junʳ
John Brown
William Edrington
John James
William Adie
Yelverton Peyton
Gerrard Hooe
Charles Alexander
Andrew Grant
John Gibson
John Chambers
Townshend Dade
William Hooe   &
John Bronaugh   Gent:
    Exᵈ
    Gen. Commissions Issued

[Page 46]

Frederick
October 23ᵈ 1769

The Right Hon. Thomas Lord
    Fairfax
Thomas Bryan Martin
Ralph Wormeley   Senʳ

Mecklenburg
Octʳ 23ᵈ 1769

Robert Munford
John Speed
Henry Delony
Edmund Taylor

[**Frederick**—Continued]
Jacob Hite
John Hite
Isaac Hite
Charles Dick
Van Swearingen
Thomas Speak
Thomas Rutherford
George Mercer
Adam Stephen
Burr Harrison   Quorum
Charles Smith
John Neavill
James Wood
Thomas Swearingen
Matthew Harrison
Angus McDonald
Charles Mynn Thruston
Samuel Washington
John McDonald
Taverner Beale
Warner Washington   &
William Miller   Junr   Gent:
    Ex^d

[**Mecklenburg**—Continued]
John Camp
Benjamin Baird
Thomas Erskine
John Potter
John Cox
Sir Peyton Skipwith Baronet Quo:
John Speed   Junr
Samuel Hopkins
Robert Alexander
William Davis
David Christopher
Joshua Mabry
Tignal Jones   &
Jacob Royster   Gent
    Ex^d

[Page 47]

Prince George
26th Octr 1769

Richard Bland
Samuel Gordon
Peter Poythress
Alexander Morrison
William Starke
Theophilus Field
Nathaniel Raines
Sir Peyton Skipwith   Bart
Peter Eppes
Nathaniel Harrison   Junr   Q.
John Poythress   Junr
James Murray
Benjamin Harrison   Junr
Patrick Ramsay
Richard Kidder Meade
Edmund Ruffin   Junr
Thomas Harris
John Gilliam   Junr
Peter Randolph Bland   &
Hubbard Wyatt   Gent.
    Exam^d
    Genl Com. iss^d

Dinwiddie
Novr 17 1769

John Jones
Robert Bolling
Bolling Stark
George Smith   Junr
Robert Walker
William Watkins
William Glascock
Herbert Haynes   Quo.
William Withers
David Walker
Abraham Smith
James Greenway
James Walker
Edward Wyatt
Thomas Scott   &
John Banister
    Ex^d

[Page 48]

Fauquier
Novr 7th 1769

Thomas Harrison
Joseph Blackwell
William Blackwell
William Eustace
William Grant
Thomas Marshall
Armistead Churchill
William Edmonds
Jeremiah Darnall
Joseph Hudnall
James Scott
James Bell   Quo.
John Moffett
Richard Chichester
John Blackwell
Jonathan Gibson
Wm Ball
Martin Picket
Henry Peyton
William Harrison
George Boswell
John Chilton   &
Charles Chinn
   Ex^d

Goochland
Novr 8th 1769

Thomas Bolling
John Bolling
Thomas Fleming
Tarlton Fleming
William Mitchell
Thomas Randolph
Joseph Woodson
John Woodson
Jesse Payne
William Harrison   Quor:
Thomas Underwood
William Pryor
George Payne   the younger
John Hopkins
Leonard Price
Thomas Harrison
Archer Payne
William Royster   Gent:
   Ex^d

[Page 49]

Charlotte
Novr 15th 1769

Paul Carrington
Clement Read
Thomas Read
Thomas Boulden
Matthew Marrable
James Hunt
James Taylor
Thomas Bedford
William Goode
David Caldwell
Elisha White
Thomas Spencer
Joseph Morton   Quo.
John White
Henry Isbell
Edward Mosby
James Venable
Josiah Morton

Sussex
Novr 27th 1769

John Mason
Nicholas Massenburg   dead
Lawrence Gibbons
David Mason
Thomas Vaughan   She^r
Michael Blow
Nathaniel Wych
Henry Gee
James Jones
John Cargill
John Mason   Junr
William Parham   Quo.
Richard Parker
John Walker
William Blunt
Ephraim Parham
Solomon Graves
Jesse Williamson

[**Charlotte**—Continued]
James Boulden
Richard Booker
William Price
James Watkins
Thomas Carter
Joseph Moore
William Morton
Stephen Bedford   &
John Fuqua   Gent.

[**Sussex**—Continued]
James Bell
George Booth
John Hunt   &
George Rieves   Gent.

[Page 50]

Amherst
Novr 27th 1769

William Cabell   Junr
James Nevil
Daniel Burford
George Stoval   Junr
Cornelius Thomas
John Rose
Francis Meriwether
James Dillard
Zachariah Taliaferro   Quo
Hugh Rose
Daniel Gaines
Ambrose Rucker
Charles Rodes
Alexander Reid   Junr
Thomas Wiatt
Roderick McCullock
David Crawford   &
William Horsley   Gent.

King & Queen
Decr 19 1769

Richard Tunstall
Philip Rootes
George Brooke
John Ware
Clack Rowe
William Fleet
Armistead Bird
Tunstall Banks
Baylor Walker
William Lyne
Thomas Coleman   Quor:
William Todd
James Dickie
Robinson Daingerfield
Lyne Shackleford
Richard Tunstall   J^r
William Taliaferro
Gregory Smith
John Tayloe Corbin
Nathaniel Carpenter   &
John Lyne   Gent

[Page 51]

Princess Anne
December 22nd 1769

James Kempe
Edward Hack Moseley
Anthony Walke
Tully Robinson   dead
John Whitehurst   dead
David McClanahan   dead
John Ackiss

Botetourt
Decr 22^d 1769

Andrew Lewis
Richard Woods
Robert Brackenridge
William Preston
John Bowyer
Israel Christian
John Maxwell   Quorum

[Princess Anne—Continued]
Mitchel Phillips
Anthony Lawson
George Logan
John Hancock   Quorum   Sherif
Thomas Reynolds Walker
Edward Cannon
Edward Moseley
William Nimmo   Jun[r]
Lemuel Cornick   dead
Samuel Tennant   dead Nov[r] 1770
William Woodhouse   Sen[r]   dead
Charles Gasking   dead
William Moseley   dead
Jacob Ellegood   Gent.
   exam[d]

[Botetourt—Continued]
James Trimble
Benjamin Hawkins
David Robinson
William Fleming
George Skillern   &
Benjamin Estell   Gent.
   Exam[d]

[Page 52]

Pittsylvania
Dec[r] 22[d] 1769

James Roberts   Jun[r]
Archibald Gordon
Thomas Dillard   Jun[r]
Hugh Innes
John Donelson
Theophilus Lacy
John Wilson
Peter Copeland
John Dix
George Jefferson
Peter Perkins
Haman Critz   Quorum
John Wembish
Robert Chandler
Benjamin Langford
Chrispen Shelton
George Carter
John Owen
Richard Walding
Robert Payne
William Thomas
William Witcher
Archilus Hughes   &
John Rowland   Gent:
   Exam[d]

Brunswick
February 5th 1770

Nicholas Edmunds
Drury Stith
John Clack
William Thornton
Thomas Stith
John Jones
Sylvanus Stokes
John Coleman
Doughlas Wilkins   Quorum
George Walker
James Wall
William Edwards
Thomas Maclin
James Belfour
Henry Mounger
Benjamin Jones
Simon Turner   &
John Turner   Gent.
   Exam[d]

[Page 53]

Botetourt
March 2ᵈ 1770
Andrew Lewis
Richard Woods
Robert Brackenridge
William Preston
John Bowyer
Israel Christian
John Maxwell
James Trimble
Benjamin Hawkins
David Robinson
William Fleming
George Skillern
Benjamin Estell
William Ingles
John Howard   Quorum
Philip Love
James Robertson
William Christian
William Herbert
John Montgomery
Stephen Trigg
Robert Doage
Walter Crocket
James McGavock
Francis Smith
Andrew Woods
William Matthews
John Bowman
William McKee   &
Anthony Bledsoe   Gent.
   Examᵈ

Charlotte
May 2ᵈ 1770
Clement Reade
Matthew Marrable
James Hunt
Thomas Bedford
Thomas Spencer
Joseph Morton
John White
Henry Isbell
James Venable   Quor:
Josiah Morton
James Boulden
William Price
James Watkins
Thomas Carter
William Morton
Stephen Bedford   &
John Fuqua   Gent.
   Examᵈ

[Page 54]

Lancaster
May 4ᵗʰ 1770
Thomas Pinckard
Dale Carter
James Ball
George Heale
John Fleet
Charles Carter
William Dymer

Caroline
May 4ᵗʰ 1770
Edmund Pendleton
Robert Gilchrist
Anthony Thornton
William Tyler
James Taylor
Robert Taliaferro   Junʳ
William Parker

[**Lancaster**—Continued]
Martin Shearman
Richard Mitchell	Quorum
Thomas Bertrand Griffin
Richard Edwards
John Chinn
Edwin Conway
Jesse Ball
James Selden	&
James Ewell	Gent.
  Examined

[**Caroline**—Continued]
John Taylor
John Baynham
Lunsford Lomax	J^r
Walker Taliaferro	Quor:
James Miller
William Woodford
John Buckner
Thomas Lowry
George Taylor
John Armistead
William Buckner	J^r
Samuel Hawes
James Upshaw
John Minor	&
Jeremiah Rawlings	Gent
  Exam^d

[Page 55]

New Kent
May 7th 1770
Richard Adams
Burwell Bassett
George Webb
Lewis Webb
Francis Foster
William Marston
Thomas Adams
Foster Webb	Quor.
John Hopkins
William Massie
Peter Russell
Richard Chamberlayne
John Lewis
Richard Allen	Senr	&
William Taylor	Gent.
  Exam^d

Richmond
May 11th 1770
Landon Carter
John Smith
William Brockenbrough
John Tarpley
William Peachy
John Belfield
Robert Wormley Carter
LeRoy Griffin
Thomas Glascock
Williamson Ball
Francis Lightfoot Lee	Quor.
William Miskell
Charles McCarty
Richard Barnes
William Colston
John Sydnor
John Suggett
Christopher Lawson	&
Charles Fauntleroy	Gent.

[Page 56]

Surry
May 11th 1770
Hartwell Cocke
John Cocke: Junr
William Brown
John White

Southampton
May 11th 1770
Joseph Gray
Jesse Brown
Albridgton Jones
James Ridley

[Surry—Continued]

James Rodwell Bradby
Nicholas Faulcon　Junr
Carter Crawford
Thomas Bailey　Quo.
William Drew
John Watkins
William Ruffin
William Allen
Nathaniel Harrison
Allen Cocke　&
Charles Harrison　Gent.
　Ex^d

[Southampton—Continued]

Peter Butts
Thomas Williamson
Nicholas Maget
James Jones
James Day Ridley　Quor.
Charles Briggs
Benjamin Ruffin　Junr
Edwin Gray
Thomas Blunt
Nathaniel Ridley
William Blunt
Charles Taylor
Thomas Edmonds　&
William Thomas　Gent.
　Ex^d

[Page 57]

King George
May 11th 1770

Thomas Jett
Charles Carter
Samuel Skinker
William Rowley　dead
William Newton
William Robinson
Anthony Strother　Junr
Arthur Morson
Horatia Dade
William Champe
Thomas Hodge
John Champe　dead
William Thornton　Quor:
Thomas Landrum　clk.　dead
James Buchannon
Thomas Hord　Junr
Thomas Beny
John Triplett
John Skinker
John Carter
George Thornton
John Taliaferro
Burket Davenport
Lawrence Ashton
Hancock Lee　&
William Allison　Gent.
　Ex^d

Augusta
June the 8th [1770 date torn]

Silas Hart
Andrew Lewis
James Lockart
Patrick Martin
John Bowyer
John Dickinson
John Christian
Daniel Smith
Archibald Alexander
Matthew Patton
John Poage
Felix Gilbert
Abraham Smith
Lemuel McDowell
George Moffett
Francis Kerkley　Quor.
Andrew Bird
Sampson Matthews
Alexander McClenachan
William Bowyer
Matthew Harrison
John McClenachan
George Matthews
Michael Bowyer
James McDowell
Alexander Robertson
John Gratton

[Augusta—Continued]
John Hays
Thomas Huggart
John Stuart
James Craig &
Elijah McClenachan   Gent.
Exam^d

[Page 58]

[Page torn]
[Sout]hampton
30th May 1770
[Jo]seph Gray
Jesse Brown
[Al]bridgton Jones
[Jam]es Ridley
[Pe]ter Butts
[Tho]mas Williamson
Nicholas Maget
[Henr]y Taylor
[Ch]arles Cosby
James Jones
James Day Ridley   Quor:
Charles Briggs
Benjamin Ruffin   Junr
Edwin Gray
Thomas Blunt
Nathaniel Ridley
William Blunt
Charles ·Taylor
Thomas Edmonds   &
William Thomas   Gent.
Exam^d

Halifax
June 14th 1770
Nathaniel Terry
Robert Wooding
William Stokes
William Hoskins
James Bates
Walter Coles
Thomas Yuille
John Lewis
Radford Maxey   Quor.
John Orril Tunstall
George Boyd
James Turner
George Muter
Evan Ragland
Henry Hopson
Isaac Coles
William McDaniel   and
Edward Wade   Gent.
Exam^d

[Page 59]

Surry
May 30th 1770
Hartwell Cocke
John Cocke   Junr
William Brown
John White
James Rodwell Bradby
Nicholas Faulcon   Junr
Carter Crawford
Thomas Bailey   Quor.
William Drew
John Watkins
William Ruffin
Etheldred Gray

Fairfax
June 13th 1770
John West
George Mason
Daniel McCarty
John Carlyle
William Ramsay
Charles Broadwater
John West   Junr
Bryan Fairfax
Sampson Darrell   Quor.
Henry Gunnell
Robert Adam
William Payne

[Surry—Continued]
William Allen
Nathaniel Harrison
Allen Cocke   and
Charles Harrison   Gent.
   Exam[d]

Hanover
June 21st 1770
John Henry   dead
Richard Johnson   dead
John Snelson
Essex William Winston
Nathaniel West Dandridge
John Syme
John Boswell   removed
Samuel Overton   dead
Henry Gilbert   removed
John Meriwether
William Macon   Jun[r]
Meriwether Skelton
John Starke   Quor
Nelson Berkley
Francis Smith   dead
Samuel Meredith
Thomas Garland
Garland Anderson
Charles Crenshaw
Geddes Winston
Peter Fontaine   dead
Benjamin Anderson
John Smith   dead
John Lawrence   &
John Robinson   Gent.
   Ex[d]

Augusta
October 25th 1770.
Silas Hart
James Lockart
Patrick Martin
John Dickinson
John Christian
Daniel Smith
Archibald Alexander
John Poage
Felix Gilbert

[Fairfax—Continued]
William Adams
Hector Ross
Alexander Henderson
George Washington   and
Edward Payne   Gent.
   Exam[d]

[Page 60]

Warwick
October 25th 1770
Henry Scasbrook
William Harwood
William Digges
William Dudley
Benjamin Wills
Harwood Jones
John Jones
Francis Jones
William Langhorn   Quor
Francis Leigh
Servant Jones
Thomas Haynes
Robert Lucas
Hind Russell
James Dowsing
James Roscow
John Wills   &
Edward Harwood   Gent:
   Ex[d]
      Gen[l] Com: of Oyer & Term:
      iss[d]

[Page 61]

Westmoreland
  –   Oct: 25th 1770.
Samuel Oldham
James Berryman
William Berryman
John Martin
Richard Henry Lee
Richard Lee
Archibald Campbell
James Blair   dead
Benjamin Weeks

[Augusta—Continued]
Abraham Smith
Lemuel McDowell
George Moffett
Francis Kirkley
Andrew Bird
Sampson Matthews
Alexander McClenachan
William Bowyer   Quor.
Matthew Harrison
John McClenachan
George Matthews
Michael Bowyer
James McDowell
Alexander Robertson
John Gratton
John Hayes
Thomas Huggart
James Craig
Elijah McClenachan
William Lewis
James Ewing
John Frogg
Josiah Davidson
Wm. Tees   &
John Skidmore   Gent
   Ex^d

[Westmoreland—Continued]
John Turberville   Quor
John Augustine Washington
Thomas Chilton
William Bernard
Philip Smith
George Turberville
Daniel McCarty
William Pierce
Joseph Pierce
Joseph Lane   &
Fleet Cox   Gent:
   Ex^d

[Page 62]

Prince William
Oct: 31st 1770.
Henry Lee
James Nisbett
Henry Peyton
James Scott   Clk.
Howson Hooe
Foushee Tebbs
William Tebbs
Thomas Lawson
Lewis Renoe
William Carr   Quor:
John Hooe
Lynaugh Helm
Daniel Payne
Thomas Blackburn
Matthew Whitinge
Spence Grayson
William Alexander
Jesse Ewell
William Cocke   &
Thomas Montgomerie   Gent
   Ex^d

Lunenburg
Novr 9th 1770
Lyddal Bacon
Joseph Williams
Thomas Tabb
David Garland
Abraham Murry
Henry Blagrave
Christopher Billups
Thomas Chambers
Thomas Winn   Quor
Richard Claiborne
John Ragsdale
Jonathan Pattason   Junr
Charles Hamlin
Everard Dowsing
Lodowick Farmer
Thomas Pettus
Elisha Bettes   &
Samuel Garland   Gent
   Ex^d

[Page 63]

Henrico
Nov[r] 8th 1770
Richard Randolph
William Lewis
Samuel Duval
Bowler Cocke   Jun[r]
Ryland Randolph
Isaac Younghusband
Joseph Lewis
Richard Adams   Quor:
Daniel Price   Jun[r]
George Cox
Nathaniel Wilkinson
William Randolph
Peter Winston
Turner Southall
James Powell Cocke   &
John Hailes   Gent
  Ex[d]

Bedford
November 8th 1770
John Phelps
Robert Ewing
Charles Talbot
William Mead
Samuel Hairstone
Richard Stith
Joseph Rentfro
Jeremiah Early
Francis Callaway
William Trigg
John Fitz Patrick
Thomas Watkins   Q
Bowker Smith
Guy Smith
James Callaway
Charles Lynch
Francis Thorp
John Talbot
Gross Scruggs
Christopher Lynch
Robert Cowan   &
James Donald   Gent.
  Exam[d]

[Page 64]

Accomack
Feb[r] 1st 1771
Littleton Scarburgh Major
Thomas Parramore
William Bagg
Covington Corbin
Thomas Riley
Isaac Smith
Tully Robinson Wise
John Watts
Isaac Dunton
James Arbuckle
William Selby   Quo:
John Wise
Southy Simpson
Daniel Gore
Henry Fletcher
William Williams
John Smith
Thomas Teackle   Jun[r]

New Kent
March 4th 1771
Richard Adams
Burwell Bassett
George Webb
Lewis Webb
Francis Foster
William Marston
Thomas Adams
Foster Webb   or
John Hopkins   Quo:
William Massie
Peter Russell
Richard Chamberlayne
John Lewis
William Taylor
John Armistead
Richard Allen
Robert Bowis   &
Richard Allen   Jun[r]   Gent.

[**Accomack**—Continued]
George Stewart
Walter Hatton
Andrew Newton &
David Bowman Gent:
  Ex^d

[Page 65]

Prince George
April 17th 1771
Richard Bland
Samuel Gordon
Peter Poythress
Richard Bland Junr
Alexander Morrison
William Starke
Theophilus Field
Nathaniel Raines
Peter Eppes
Theoderick Bland J^r
Nathaniel Harrison Junr Quorum
John Poythress Junr
Benjamin Harrison Junr
Patrick Ramsay
Richard Kidder Meade
Edmund Ruffin Junr
Thomas Harris
John Gilliam Junr
Peter Randolph Bland &
Hubbard Wyatt Gent.
  Exam^d

Albemarle
April 17th 1771
William Harris
Henry Martin
Mosias Jones
Nicholas Lewis
Nicholas Meriwether
John Henderson Junr
Charles Lewis
John Scott
William Burton Quorum
John Ware
Thomas Jefferson
John Walker
Charles Lewis Junr
Isaac Davis
David Rodes
Edward Carter
Isaac Coles
Roger Thompson &
John Cole Gent.
  Exam^d

Accomack
April 17th 1771
Thomas Parramore
Covington Corbin
Thomas Riley
Isaac Smith
Tully Robinson Wise
John Watts
Isaac Dunton
James Arbuckle
William Selby Quorum
Southy Simpson
Henry Fletcher
William Williams
John Smith
Thomas Teackle Junr
George Stewart
Walter Hatton
Andrew Newton &
David Bowman Gent:
  Exam^d

[Page 66]

Loudoun County
26th April 1771
Thomson Mason
Francis Lightfoot Lee
James Hamilton
Nicholas Minor
Josias Clapham
George West
Francis Peyton
John McElhaney
James Lane
Craven Peyton
Philip Noland
Leven Powell   Quorum
John Minor
William Douglass
Thomas Lewis
Simon Triplett
Stephen Donaldson
William Smith
George Sumners
Fleming Patterson
James Coleman
Charles Brent   &
Samuel Love   Gent.
   Exam^d

Brunswick
April 30th 1771
Nicholas Edmunds
Drury Stith   dead
John Clack
William Thornton
Thomas Stith
John Jones
Sylvanus Stokes
John Coleman
Thomas Simmons
Douglass Wilkins
George Walker   Quo:
James Wall
William Edwards
Thomas Maclin
James Belfour
Henry Mounger
Benjamin Jones
John Flood Edmunds
Richard Elliott
Augustine Willis   &
John Powell   Gent
   Ex^d

Lancaster
April 30th 1771
Thomas Pinckard
James Ball
Dale Carter
John Fleet
Charles Carter
Richard Mitchell
Richard Edwards
John Chinn   Quor
Edwin Conway
Jesse Ball
James Selden
James Ewell
Hugh Brent
John Taylor
Burges Smith   &
Thomas Lawson   Gent.
   Exam^d

[Page 67]

Northumberland
May 1st 1771
Richard Hull
Thos Gaskins
John Eustace
Spencer Mottrom Ball
Rodham Kenner
Winder Kenner
David Ball   Jun.
Charles Bell
Peter Presly Thornton   Quor:
John Smith   Junr
Lindsey Opie
Joseph Ball
Kenner Cralle
James Ball
Thomas Gaskins   Junr
William Taylor   &
Griffin Fountleroy   Gent.
   Exam^d

[Page 68]

Sussex
May 4th 1771

John Mason
Nicholas Massenburg
David Mason
Thomas Vaughan
Michael Blow
Nathaniel Wyche
Henry Gee
James Jones
William Parham
Richard Parker   Quor:
John Walker
William Blunt
Robert Pettway
Nathaniel Harrison
Richard Blunt
Robert Jones
Thomas Peele
John Peters
Lawrence Gibbons   Jr   &
Isham Smith   Gent.
     Exd

Henrico
May 4th 1771

Richard Randolph
William Lewis
Samuel DuVal
Ryland Randolph
Isaac Younghusband
Joseph Lewis
Richard Adams
William Randolph   Quor:
Daniel Price   Junr
George Cox
Nathaniel Wilkinson
Peter Winston
Turner Southall
James Powell Cocke   &
John Hailes   Gent.
     Exd

[Page 69]

Halifax
May 8th 1771

Nathaniel Terry
Robert Wooding
James Bates
Walter Coles
Thomas Yuille
John Orrill Tunstall
George Boyd   Quor:
James Turner
Isaac Coles
William McDaniel
Edward Wade
William Sims
Micajah Watkins   &
Nathaniel Hunt   Gent:
     Exd

Charlotte
May 8th 1771

James Hunt
Thomas Bedford
Thomas Spencer
Joseph Morton
John White
James Venable
Josiah Morton
James Boulden
William Price
Thomas Carter   Quor:
William Morton
John Brent
Sion Spencer
Joel Watkins
Silvanus Stokes
Joseph Friend
Matthew Watson
Mackerness Goode   Jr
Joseph Moore   &
John Pettus   Gent.
     Exd

[Page 70]

Mecklenburg	Louisa
May 8th 1771	May 11th 1771
Robert Munford	Thomas Johnson
John Speed	Robert Anderson
Henry Delony	William Johnson
Edmund Taylor	Thomas Ballard Smith
John Camp	Nathaniel Pope
Thomas Erskine	George Thompson
John Potter	James Overton
John Cox	Samuel Ragland
Sir Peyton Skipwith Bart:	Thomas Poindexter
John Speed Junr Quor:	Thomas Johnson Junr
Robert Alexander	James Meriwether
William Davis	Richard Anderson
David Christopher	Waddy Thompson Quor:
Joshua Mabry	William Phillips
Jacob Royster	William Meriwether
Lewis Burwell Jr	Charles Smith
Samuel Bugg	Nathaniel Garland
Reuben Vaughan	Benjamin Lewis
Samuel Young &	William Garrett
Anselmn Bugg Gent:	Samuel Temple
Exd	William White
	William Anderson
	Nathaniel Anderson
	James Dabney
	John Daniel &
	John Poindexter Gent:
	Exd

[Page 71]

Southampton	Albemarle
12th June 1771	12th June 1771
Joseph Gray dead	William Harris
Jesse Brown	Mosias Jones
Albridgton Jones	John Henderson Jr
James Ridley	William Burton
Peter Butts	John Ware
Thomas Williamson	John Walker
Nicholas Maget	Isaac Davis
Henry Taylor	David Rodes
Charles Cosby	Roger Thompson
James Jones	John Coles Quo
James Day Ridley Quor	Matthew Maury
Charles Briggs	Charles Clay
Benjamin Ruffin Jr	George Gilmer
Edwin Gray	James Quarles

[Southampton—Continued]
Thomas Blunt
Nathaniel Ridley
William Blunt
Charles Taylor
Thomas Edmunds   &
William Thomas   Gent.
  Ex^d

King William
12th June 1771
Francis West
Bernard Moore
Thomas Chamberlayne
Richard Squire Taylor
John Quarles
Philip Whitehead Claiborne
Carter Braxton
Roger Gregory   Quo^r
John West
Owen Gwathmey
Ferdinando Leigh
John Hill
Robert Brooke
William Aylett
William Burnett Brown   &
John Roan   Gent
  Ex^d

Sussex
July 13th 1771
John Mason
Nicholas Massenburg   dead
David Mason
Thomas Vaughan
Michael Blair
Nathaniel Wyche
Henry Gee
James Jones
William Parham
Richard Parker
John Walker   Quo
William Blunt
George Boothe

[Albemarle—Continued]
Thomas Carr
William Henry
James Adams
Charles Wingfield   &
William Tandy
  Ex^d

[Page 72]

Accomack
13th June 1771
Thomas Parramore
William Bagge
Covington Corbin
Thomas Riley
Isaac Smith
Tully Robinson Wise
John Watts
Isaac Dunton
James Arbuckle
William Selby   Quo
Southy Simpson
Henry Fletcher
William Williams
John Smith
Thomas Teackle   J^r
George Stewart
Walter Hatton
Andrew Newton   &
David Bowman   Gent
  Ex^d   Ch

[Page 73]

King William
17 July 1771
Francis West
James Quarles
Bernard Moore
Thomas Chamberlayne
Richard Squire Taylor
John Quarles
Philip Whitehead Claiborne
Carter Braxton
Roger Gregory   Q
John West
Owen Gwathmey
Ferdinando Leigh
John Hill

[Sussex—Continued]
Robert Pettway
Nathaniel Harrison
Richard Blunt
Robert Jones
Thomas Peele
John Peters
Lawrence Gibbons   J^r &
Isham Smith   Gent.
    Ex^d Ch

[King William—Continued]
Robert Brooke
William Aylett
John Roan
William Burnett Brown
    Ex^d Ch

Dinwiddie
July 17th 1771
John Jones
Robert Bolling
Bolling Starke
George Smith   J^r
Robert Walker
William Watkins
William Glascock
Herbert Haynes
William Withers   Quo
David Walker
Abraham Smith
James Greenway
James Walker
Edward Wyatt
Thomas Scott
John Banister   &
Daniel Claiborne   Gent.
    Ex^d Ch

[Page 74]

Botetourt
July 17th 1771
Andrew Lewis
Richard Woods
Robert Brackenridge
William Preston
John Bowyer
Israel Christian
John Maxwell
James Trimble
Benjamin Hawkins
David Robinson
William Fleming
George Skillern
Benjamin Estell
William Ingles
John Howard
Philip Love
James Robertson

Northumberland
July 18th 1771
Richard Hull
Thomas Gaskins
John Eustace
Joseph McAdam
Spencer Mottrom Ball
Rodham Kenner
Winder Kenner
Charles Fallen
David Ball   J^r
Charles Bell
John Smith   J^r
Lindsey Opie
Peter Presly Thornton   Quo
Joseph Ball
William Davenport
James Ball
Thomas Gaskins   J^r

[Botetourt—Continued]
William Christian   Quor
William Herbert
John Montgomery
Stephen Trigg
Robert Doage
Walter Crocket
James McGavock
Francis Smith
Andrew Woods
William Matthews
John Bowman
William McKee
Anthony Bledsoe
James Thompson
John Stewart
John Robinson
John Venbebber   &
Matthew Arbuckle   Gent   Ch
  Ex^d

[Northumberland—Continued]
William Taylor
Griffin Fauntleroy
Charles Lee
Kenner Cralle   &
William Eskridge   Gent.   Ch
  Ex^d

[Page 75]

Sussex
November 6th 1771
John Mason
Nicholas Massenburg   dead
David Mason
Thomas Vaughan
Michael Blow
Nathaniel Wyche
Henry Gee
James Jones
William Parham
Richard Parker
John Walker   Quor:
William Blunt
George Boothe
Robert Pettway
Nathaniel Harrison
Richard Blunt
Robert Jones
Thomas Peele
John Peters
Lawrence Gibbons   J^r   &
Isham Smith   Gent:
  Ex^d

Dinwiddie
November 6th 1771
John Jones
Robert Bolling
Bolling Starke
George Smith   J^r
Robert Walker
William Watkins
William Glascock
Herbert Haynes
William Withers   Quor:
David Walker
Abraham Smith
James Greenway
James Walker
Edward Wyatt
Thomas Scott
John Banister   &
Daniel Claiborne   Gent:
  Ex^d

[Page 76]

York
Novr 8th 1771

Peyton Randolph   Esq.
Dudley Digges
William Allen
Robert Shield
John Prentis
Robert Smith
John Blair
Thomas Nelson   Junr
David Jameson ·
William Nelson   Junr
Anthony Robinson   Junr   Quor ;
William Graves
James Cocke
Starkey Robinson
William Stevenson
James Burwell
Jaquelin Ambler
William Digges   J^r
Augustine Moore
Lawrence Smith   Junr
Hugh Nelson   &
John Dixon   Gent
    Exam^d

Surry
Decr 12th 1771

Hartwell Cocke
John Cocke   Junr
William Brown
John White
James Rodwell Bradby
Nicholas Faulcon   **Junr**
Carter Crawford
William Drew   Quor.
John Watkins
William Ruffin
Etheldred Gray
William Hart
William Allen
Nathaniel Harrison
Allen Cocke   &
Charles Harrison   **Gent**
    Ex^d

[Page 77]

Buckingham
March 1772

Samuel Jordan
John Nicholas
Robert Bolling
George Hooper
Jacob Lindsey
John Cabell
Jeremiah Whitney
Charles Pattison
William Cannon   Quor
Charles May
John Johns
Samuel Taylor
Anthony Winston
Henry Bell
John Bernard
Thomas Patteson   &
Archibald Bolling   Gent
    Ex^d

New Kent
8th April 1772

Richard Adams
Burwell Bassett
George Webb
Lewis Webb
Francis Foster
William Marston
Thomas Adams
Foster Webb
John Hopkins   Quor:
William Massie
Peter Russell
Richard Chamberlayne
John Lewis
William Taylor
John Armistead
Richmond Allen
John Bowis   &
Richard Allen   **Junr**   **Gent**
    Ex^d

[Page 78]

Dunmore
April 17ᵗʰ 1772

Burr Harrison
Taverner Beale
Joseph Pugh
Francis Slaughter
James McKay
Henry Nelson
Abraham Keller   Quor:
John Tipton
Caleb Odell
Jonathan Langdon
Abraham Bowman
William Moore
George Ruddell
Jacob Holeman   &
Alexander Machir   Gent.
    Exᵈ

Frederick
April 17ᵗʰ 1772

The Rᵗ Hon. Thoˢ Lord Fairfax
Thoˢ Bryan Martin
John Hite
Isaac Hite
Charles Smith
James Wood   Quor.
Angus McDonald
Charles Mynn Thruston   Clk.
John McDonald
Warner Washington
William Miller   Junʳ
Marquis Calmees   &
Isaac Lane   Gent.
    Exᵈ

[Page 79]

Berkeley
April 17ᵗʰ 1772

Ralph Wormeley
Jacob Hite
Van Swearingen
Thomas Rutherford
Adam Stephen
John Neville
Thomas Swearingen
Samuel Washington   Quor
James Nourse
William Little
Robert Stephen
John Briscoe
Hugh Lyle
James Strode
William Morgan
Robert Stogdon
James Seaton
Robert Willis   &
Thomas Robinson   Gent.
    Exᵈ

Accomack
May 9ᵗʰ 1772

Thomas Parramore
William Bagge
Covington Corbin
Thomas Riley
Isaac Smith
Tully Robinson Wise
John Watts
Isaac Dunton
James Arbuckle
William Selby   Quorum
Henry Fletcher
William Williams
John Smith
Thomas Teackle   Junʳ
George Stewart
Walter Hatton
Andrew Newton   &
David Bowman   Gent.
    Examined

[Page 80]

Prince Edward
11ᵗʰ May 1772
John Nash
Abraham Venable
Joel Watkins
John Nash   Junʳ
Thomas Scott
Thomas Haskins
James Scott
Peter LeGrand
John Leigh   Quor:
Henry Watkins
Peter Johnston
John Morton
Charles Venable
Nathaniel Venable
Benjamin Haskins
William Booker   &
Philemon Halcombe   Gent.
     Exᵈ

Charles City
June 11ᵗʰ 1772
Benjamin Harrison
William Hardyman
John Jacob Coignan Dansie
William Acrill
William Edloe
Philip Par Edmondson
Littlebury Cocke
William Green Munford   Quor
Thomas Holt
William Rickman
Benjamin Harrison   Jʳ
Freeman Walker
John Woddrop
Robert Harrison
David Minge   &
William Christian   Gent.
     Exᵈ

[Page 81]

New Kent
June 10ᵗʰ 1772
Richard Adams
Burwell Bassett
George Webb
Lewis Webb
Francis Foster
William Marston
Thomas Adams
Foster Webb
John Hopkins   Quorum
William Massie
Peter Russell
Richard Chamberlayne
John Lewis
William Taylor
John Armistead
Richmond Allen
Robert Bowis   &
Richard Allen   Jʳ   Gent:
     Examᵈ

Caroline
June 10ᵗʰ 1772
Edmund Pendleton
Robert Gilchrist
Anthony Thornton
James Taylor
Robert Taliaferro   Junʳ
William Parker
Walker Taliaferro
James Miller
William Woodford
John Buckner
Thomas Lowry   Quorum
John Armistead
William Buckner   Jʳ
Samuel Hawes
James Upshaw
John Minor
Gawin Corbin
William Harrison
Roger Quarles
George Guy   &
Anthony New
     Exᵈ

[Page 82]

[page torn]
[Halifax]
July 27th 1772

Nathaniel Terry
Robert Wooding
James Bates
Walter Coles
Thomas Yuille
John Orrill Tunstall
George Boyd
James Turner
Isaac Coles
William McDaniel   Quorum
Edward Wade
William Sims
Micajah Watkins
Nathaniel Hunt
James Coleman
Moses Fontaine
William Britton
Marmaduke Stanfield   &
Matthew Sims
   Examined
      So far charged

Hampshire
Oct. 15th 1772

Henry Vanmetre
Abraham Hite
Garrett Vanmetre
Jonathan Heath
Robert Parker
Abraham Johnston
Enoch Tunis
Stephen Ruddell
George Wilson   Quorum
John Forman
Simon Taylor
William McCracken
Joseph Neaville
Humphry Fullerton
Philip Ross
William Vause
James Claypole   Junr   &
Isaac Cox   Gent   Ch

[Page 83]

Dinwiddie
Octr 15th 1772

John Jones
George Smith   Junr
William Glascock
William Withers
David Walker
Abraham Smith
James Greenway
James Walker
Thomas Scott   Quorum
John Banister
Daniel Claiborne
John Jones   Junr
Duncan Rose
Alexander Shaw
Robert Newsum
Henry Lockhead   &
Joseph Jones   Gent.

Gloucester
Octr 30th 1772

James Hubbard
Francis Tomkies
Thomas Whitinge
Lewis Burwell
John Hughes
Thomas Smith
Jonathan Watson
John Page   Junior
William Armstead   Quorum
Mann Page   Junior
James Hubbard   Junior
Kemp Whitinge
George Booth
Charles Tomkies
Warner Lewis   Junior
John Cooke   Junior
Francis Willis   Junr
George Booth   Junior   &
John Thruston   Gent.
   Exd   Ch

[Page 84]

King & Queen
October 17th 1772

Richard Tunstall
Philip Rootes
George Brooke
John Ware
Clack Wroe
William Fleet
Tunstall Banks
William Lyne
Thomas Coleman
William Todd
John Tayloe Corbin   Quorum
James Dickie
Lyne Shackleford
William Taliaferro
Nathaniel Carpenter
John Lyne
Robert Hill
William Griffin
Edward Hill
Benjamin Robinson   &
William Black   Gent.
   Ch   Examined

James City
Novr 6th 1772

John Randolph Esqr   out of Colony
Richard Taliaferro
Lewis Burwell   declined
Philip Johnson
Robert Carter Nicholas
John Tyler   dead
Dudley Richardson
William Norvell
William Spratley   Quorum
Banjamin Weldon
Richard Taliaferro   Junr
John Cooper
Haldenby Dixon   left sd cnty
Joseph Eggleston
William Holt
Lewis Burwell   Junr
Nathaniel Burwell   &
Champion Travis   Gent.
   Ex^d   Ch

[Page 85]

Augusta
November 6th 1772

Silas Hart
James Lockart
John Dickinson
John Christian
Daniel Smith
Archibald Alexander
John Poage
Felix Gilbert
Abraham Smith
Samuel McDowell
George Moffett
Sampson Matthews
Alexander McClenachan
William Bowyer   Quorum
Matthew Harrison
John McClenachan
George Matthews
Michael Bowyer

Southampton
November 6th 1772

Albridgton Jones
James Ridley
Peter Butts
Thomas Williamson
Nicholas Maget
Henry Taylor
James Day Ridley
Charles Briggs   Quorum
Benjamin Ruffin   Junr
Edwin Gray
Thomas Blunt
Nathaniel Ridley
William Blunt
Samuel Browne   &
Elias Herring   Gent:
   Ex^d   Ch

[Augusta—Continued]
Alexander Robertson
John Gratton
John Hayes
Thomas Huggart
James Craig
Elijah McClenachan
John Frogg
Josiah Davidson
William Tees   &
John Skidmore   Gent:
  Ex^d   Ch

[Page 86]

Berkeley
Novr 6th 1772
Ralph Wormeley
Jacob Hite
Van Swearingen
Thomas Rutherford
Adam Stephen
Thomas Swearingen
Samuel Washington
James Nourse
William Little
Robert Stephen   Quorum
James Strode
William Morgan
Robert Stogdon
James Seaton
Robert Carter Willis   &
Robert Tabb   Gent.
  Ex^d   Ch

Stafford
Novr 6th 1772
Thomas Ludwell Lee
Henry Fitzhugh
Francis Thornton
John Stewart
John Washington
Samuel Selden
Gowry Waugh
William Brent   Quorum
John Alexander
Robert Washington
John Brown
John James
Yelverton Peyton
Townshend Dade
William Hooe   &
Charles Carter   Gent.
  Ex^d   Ch

[Page 87]

Fincastle
December 1st 1772
William Preston
William Ingles
William Christian
John Montgomery
Stephen Trigg
Robert Doake
Walter Crockett
James McGavock   Quorum
Anthony Bledsoe
James Thompson
Arthur Campbell
William Russell

Nansemond
December 9th 1772
Willis Riddick
Thomas Godwin
Anthony Holliday
Henry Riddick
Jeremiah Godwin
Edward Wright
Benjamin Baker
William Shepherd
Samuel Cohoon
John King
David Meade   Quorum
Thomas Jack

[Fincastle—Continued]
Benjamin Estill
Samuel Crockett &
Alexander McKee   Gent.
  Examined   Ch

[Nansemond—Continued]
William Cowper
Thomas Godwin   Junr
Michael King
Jonathan Godwin
William Pugh
Solomon Shepherd   Junr
Kinchin Godwin
Anthony Godwin
Josiah Riddick   Junr   &
John Cole   J^r   Gentlemen
  Ex^d   Ch

[Page 88]

Isle of Wight
Dec. 9th 1772

James Bridger
Daniel Herring
Nicholas Parker
John Scasbrook Wills
George Purdie
Richard Hardy
Brewer Godwin
Thomas Pierce   Quorum
John Lawrence
Timothy Tynes
Arthur Smith
Nathaniel Fleming
Goodrich Wilson
James Allen Bridger
Benjamin Eley   &
Daniel Herring   Junr   Gent.
  Ex^d
    So far charged

New Kent
March 9th 1773

Richard Adams
Burwell Bassett
George Webb
Lewis Webb
Francis Foster
William Marston
Foster Webb
John Hopkins   Quorum
William Massie
Richard Chamberlayne
John Lewis
Thomas Massie
James Underwood
John Timberlake
Edwin Waddill   &
Andrew Anderson   Gentlemen
  Ex^d & Charged

[Page 89]

Stafford
March 11th 1773

Thomas Ludwell Lee
Henry Fitzhugh
Francis Thornton
William Fitzhugh
John Stewart
John Washington
Bailey Washington
Samuel Selden
Gowry Waugh
William Brent
John Alexander   Quorum

Berkeley
April 14th 1773

Ralph Wormeley   lives out of the
    County
Adam Stephen
John Neville
Samuel Washington   Shf.
Robert Stephen
Robert Carter Willis
Robert Tabb   dead
Horatio Gates
John Throckmorton   dead
Thomas Lowry   Quorum   lives
    out of the County

[Stafford—Continued]
Robert Washington
John Brown
John James
Yelverton Peyton
Townshend Dade
William Hoe   &
Charles Carter   Gent.
     Charged   Exam^d

[Berkeley—Continued]
John Cooke
John Ariss
Godwin Swift
William Patterson
Henry Whitinge
Robert Worthenton
Morgan Morgan   &
William McGaw   Gentlemen
     Ex^d & Charged

[Page 90]

Fincastle
April 30th 1773
William Preston
William Ingles
William Christian
John Montgomery
Stephen Trigg
Robert Doake
Walter Crockett
James McGavock
Anthony Bledsoe   Quorum
James Thompson
Arthur Campbell
William Russell
Benjamin Estill
Samuel Crockett
Alexander McKee
William Campbell   &
James McCorkle   Gent.
     Ch.

Spotsylvania
May 10th 1773
Fielding Lewis
Charles Dick
Beverly Winston
Joseph Brock
John Scandland Crane
William Smith
Charles Washington
Charles Yates   Q.
Robert Chew
Mann Page   Jun.
Edward Herndon
William Daingerfield
John Lewis
George Stubblefield   &
James Duncanson   Gent.
     Ex^d   Ch.

[Page 91]

Culpeper
May 10th 1773
Nathaniel Pendleton
Daniel Brown
Robert Green
William Williams
John Strother
William Brown
Joseph Wood
John Slaughter
James Barbour   Junr
Benjamin Roberts
Wm Kirtley   Quorum

Lancaster
May 10th 1773
Thomas Pinckard
James Ball
Dale Carter
John Fleet
Charles Carter
Richard Mitchell
John Chinn
Edwin Conway
Jesse Ball   Quorum
James Selden
James Ewell

[Culpeper—Continued]
James Slaughter
Henry Field   Junr
George Witherall
John Green
James Pendleton
Samuel Clayton
William Ball
Robert Throckmorton
Richard Pollard   &
Joseph Steward   Gent.
  Ex^d   Ch.

King William
May 10th 1773

Francis West
John Quarles
Carter Braxton
John West
Owen Gwathmey
John Hill
Robert Brooke
William Aylett
John Roan   Quorum
Thomas Elliott
Archibald Govan
Thomas Row
Benjamin Temple
Christopher Taliaferro
Isaac Dabney
Thomas Taylor   and
Holt Richeson   Gent:
  Exam^d   Ch. on the Couny
    [County]

Botetourt
June 11th 1773

Andrew Lewis
Robert Brackenridge
John Bowyer
John Maxwell
James Trimble
David Robinson
William Fleming
George Skillern
Benjamin Estill

[Lancaster—Continued]
Hugh Brent
John Taylor
Burgess Smith
Thomas Lawson
Burgess Ball   &
James Gordon   Gent.
  Exam^d   Ch.

[Page 92]

Accomack
May 10th 1773

Thomas Parramore
William Bagge   dead
Covington Corbin
Thomas Riley   dead
Isaac Smith
Tully Robinson Wise
John Watts
Isaac Dunton   dead
James Arbuckle
William Silby
Henry Fletcher   Quorum
William Williams
John Smith
Thomas Teackle   Junr
George Stewart
Walter Hatton
Andrew Newton
David Bowman   &
Edward Kerr   Gent.
  Ex^d   Ch.

[Page 93]

Frederick
August 16th 1773

The Right Honble Thomas Lord
    Fairfax
Thomas Bryan Martin
John Hite
Isaac Hite
Angus McDonald
James Wood
Charles Smith
Charles Mynn Thruston

[Botetourt—Continued]
Philip Love
Andrew Woods
John Bowman
William McKee
John Stewart
John Vanbebber   Quorum
2 Richard May
   Thomas Bowyer
4 William Maddison
3 Patrick Lockart
   Henry Paullin
   James Templeton
1 Samuel Lewis
   Andrew Boyd
6 William McClenachan
5 John Murry
   William Heugart
   Henry Smith
   Andrew Donely   &
   James McAfee   Gent.
      Ex^d   Ch.

Culpeper.
Octr 12th 1773
Nathaniel Pendleton
Robert Green
William Williams
William Brown
Joseph Wood
John Slaughter
James Barbour
William Kirtley
James Slaughter
George Weatherall
Samuel Clayton   Junr
Henry Fry
William Knox   Quorum
French Strother
Edward Stevens
William Walker
Benjamin Roberts
John Tutt
William Thompson
Joseph Roberts
Robert Eastham   Junr
Ambrose Barbour   &
John Waugh   Gent:
   Ex^d   Ch.

[Frederick—Continued]
John MacDonald
Isaac Zane   Quorum
William Booth
Warner Washington   Jun.
John Smith
Edmund Taylor
Robert Throckmorton   &
Edward Snickers   Gent.
   Exam^d   Ch.

[Page 94]

Albemarle
Oct. 26th 1773
William Harriss
William Burton
John Ware
John Walker
Isaac Davis
David Rhodes
Roger Thompson
John Coles
James Quarles
James Adams   Quorum
William Henry
Richard Anderson
James Hopkins
George Thompson
Thomas Napier
Jesse Burton
Clifton Rhodes   &
John Marks   Gent:
   Examined   Ch.

[Page 95]

Warwick
October 26ᵗʰ 1773
William Harwood
William Digges
William Dudley
Benjamin Wills
John Jones
Francis Jones
William Langhorn
Francis Leigh
Thomas Haynes
Robert Lucas   Quorum
Hind Russell
Edward Harwood   &
Cole Digges   Gent.
   Examined   Ch.

Dunmore
October 26ᵗʰ 1773
Burr Harrison
Taverner Beale
Joseph Pugh
Francis Slaughter
Henry Nelson
Abraham Keller
John Tipton
Jonathan Langdon   Quoʳ
Abraham Bowman
Jacob Holeman
Alexander Martin
William Miller   Sen.
Thomas Allen   &
John Buck   Gent.   Ch.
   The Commission of the Peace
   for this miscarried and must
   be sent to the Clerk when the
   Governor comes to Town.

[Page 96]

Halifax
29ᵗⁿ Oct. 1773
Nathaniel Terry
Robert Wooding
James Bates
Waller Coles
Thoˢ Yuille
John Orrill Tunstall
George Boyd
James Turner
Isaac Coles
Micajah Watkins
Nathaniel Hunt
James Coleman   Quo.
Moses Fontaine
Marmaduke Stanfield
†Matthew Simms   [10 for the Q.]
John Coleman
William Lawson
Nathaniel Cocke
Elijah Hunt   &
William Terry   Gent.
   Examᵈ   Ch.

York
3ᵈ December 1773
Peyton Randolph   Esqʳ
Dudley Digges
Robert Smith
John Blair
Thomas Nelson   Junior
David Jameson
William Nelson   Junʳ
Anthony Robinson
William Graves
Starkey Robinson
Jaquelin Ambler   Quo.
William Digges   Junior
Augustine Moore
Hugh Nelson
John Dixon
John Halley Norton
Joseph Hornsby
William Reynolds   and
William Pasteur   Gent
   Examᵈ   Ch.

---

†Several of the names on this list are in the original written on the side of the column. "James Coleman" is the 9th name on the list; not the 12th, as, after the insertion of three of the names on the side, it appears above. The meaning of the note "10 for the Q" alongside the name of Matthew Simms appears to be that there are to be ten members of the quorum, of whom Matthew Simms is to be one.

[Page 97]

Augusta
December 17ᵗʰ 1773

Silas Hart
James Lockart
John Dickinson
John Christian
Daniel Smith
Archibald Alexander
John Poage
Felix Gilbert
Abraham Smith
Samuel McDowell
George Moffett
Sampson Matthews
Alexander McClenachan
William Bowyer
Matthew Harrison
John McClenachan
George Matthews
Michael Bowyer   Quorum
Alexander Robertson
John Gratton
John Hayes
Thomas Huggart
James Craig
Elijah McClenachan
John Frogg
Josiah Davidson
William Tees
John Skidmore
George Croghan
John Campbell
John Connolly
Edward Ward
Thomas Smallman
Dawsey Pentecost   &
John Gibson
     Ch.

Northumberland
Dec. [date torn off]

Richard Hull   dead
Thomas Gaskins
John Eustace
Joseph McAdam
Spencer Mottrom Ball
Rodham Kenner   dead
Winder Kenner
Charles Fallen   dead
David Ball
Peter Presley Thornton
John Smith   Junʳ
Lindsey Opie   Quorum
Joseph Ball
William Davenport
James Ball
Thomas Gaskins   Junʳ
William Taylor
Griffin Fauntleroy
Charles Lee
Kenner Cralle   and
William Eskridge   Gent
     Exᵈ   Ch.
     The member[s] from that county
     marked to be left out ‡

‡A check mark is alongside each of the following names: John Eustace, David Ball, James Ball, and Griffin Fauntleroy.

[page torn]
[Norfolk]
Decʳ 15ᵗʰ 1773

[George] Veal
James Webb
William Aitcheson
Matthew Godfrey
John Tatem

[Page 98]

Dinwiddie
Febʳ 12 1774

John Jones
Bolling Starke
George Smith   Junʳ
Robert Walker
William Watkins
William Withers

[Norfolk—Continued]
John Hutchings
Thomas Veal
Joseph Hutchings
John Portlock
Cornelius Calvert
Samuel Hopper
Goodrich Boush   Quorum
Malichi Wilson   Jun[r]
Matthew Phripp
David Porter
Thomas Newton   Jun[r]
John Wilson
John Taylor   Sen[r]
Arthur Boush
Bassett Moseley
John Brickall
Robert Taylor   &
William Smith   Gentlemen
   Ex[d]   Ch.

[Dinwiddie—Continued]
David Walker
Abraham Smith
James Greenway
Edward Wyatt
Thomas Scott
John Banister
Daniel Claiborne   Quor:
John Jones   Jun.
Duncan Rose
Alexander Shaw
Robert Newsum
Henry Lockhead   &
Joseph Jones   Gent.
   Ex[d]   Ch.

[Page 99]

Bedford

Feb[y] 28th 1774

John Phelps   dead
Robert Ewing
Charles Talbot
William Meade
Samuel Hairstone
Richard Stith
Joseph Rentfro
Jeremiah Early
Francis Callaway
William Trigg   dead
John Fitzpatrick
Thomas Watkins   dead
Bowker Smith   dead
Guy Smith
James Callaway
Charles Lynch
John Talbot
Gross Scruggs
Christopher Lynch
Robert Cowan   &
James Donald   Gent.   removed
   Exam[d]   Ch.

New Kent

Feb[y] 28th [date torn off]

Richard Adams   removed
Burwell Bassett
George Webb   removed
Francis Foster
William Marston   dead
Foster Webb
John Hopkins
William Massie
Richard Chamberlayne
John Lewis   removed
Thomas Massie   in the army
John Timberlake   Q.
Edwin Waddill
William Smith   removed
Richmond Allen   &
Richard Allen   Gent.   dead
   Ex[d]   Ch.

[Page 100]

Lancaster
May the 3ᵈ 1774
James Ball
Dale Carter
John Fleet
Charles Carter
Richard Mitchell
John Chinn
Edwin Conway
Jesse Ball
James Selden
James Ewell
Hugh Brent
John Taylor   Quorum
Burgess Smith
Thomas Lawson
Burgess Ball   &
James Gordon   Gent:
   Exᵈ

Princess Anne
May 3ᵈ 1774
James Kempe
Edward Hack Moseley
Anthony Walke
John Ackiss
Mitchell Phillips
Anthony Lawson
George Logan
John Hancock
Thomas Reynolds Walker
Edward Cannon
Edward Moseley   Quorum
William Nimmo
Jacob Ellegood
Lemuel Newton   &
Peter Singleton   Gent:
   Ch.

[Page 101]

Botetourt
May 30ᵗʰ 1774
Andrew Lewis
John Bowyer
John Maxwell
James Trimbell
David Robinson
William Fleming
George Skillern
Benjamin Estill
Philip Love
Andrew Woods
John Bowman
William McKee
Samuel Lewis
Richard May   Quorum
William Madison
John Murry
William McClanahan
James Henderson   &
Andrew Donely   Gent.   &
Adam Smyth   Clk.
   Exᵈ   Ch.

Essex
June 2ᵈ 1774
Simon Miller
Archibald Ritchie
Thomas Roane
John Upshaw
Samuel Peachy
Robert Beverley
Meriwether Smith
John Corrie
William Roane
James Edmondson
John Beale
William Woddrop   Quorum
William Smith
Augustine Moore
Thomas Waring   &
Newman Brockenbrough.   Gent.
   Exᵈ   Ch.

[Page 102]

Pittsylvania
June 16th 1774
Archibald Gordon
Hugh Innes
John Donelson
Theophilus Lacy
John Wilson
Peter Copland
John Dix
Peter Perkins
John Wimbish
Crispen Shelton
Richard Walding
William Thomas   Quorum
William Witcher
Archilaus Hughes
James Walker
Robert Hairstone
James Smith   &
John McGound
    Ch.

Brunswick
June 17th 1774
Nicholas Edmunds
John Clack
William Thornton
Thomas Stith
John Jones   Shf.
Douglass Wilkins
John Flood Edmunds
Richard Elliott
Augustine Willis
John Powell
Frederick Maclin
William Starke   Quor
George Elliott   Junr
Edward Travis   &
Benjamin Simmons   Gent.
    Exd   Ch.

[Page 103]

Buckingham
June 27th 1774
John Nicholas
Robert Bolling
George Hooper
John Cabell
Jeremiah Whitney
Charles Pattison
William Cannon
Charles May
John Johns
Henry Bell   Quorum
John Bernard
Thomas Pattison
Dolphin Drew   &
Robert Cary   Gent.
    Exd   Ch.

Augusta
December 6th 1774
Silas Hart
James Lockart
John Dickenson
John Christian
Daniel Smith
Archibald Alexander
John Poage
Felix Gilbert
Abraham Smith
Samuel McDowell
George Moffett
Sampson Matthews
Alexander McClenachan
William Bowyer
Matthew Harrison
George Matthews
Michael Bowyer
Alexander Robertson
John Gratton
John Hayes
Thomas Huggart

[Augusta—Continued]

James Craig
Elijah McClenachan
John Frogg
Josiah Davidson
William Tees
John Skidmore
George Croghan
John Campbell
John Connolly
Edward Ward   Quor:
Thomas Smallman
Dawsey Pentecost
John Gibson
Wm. Crawford
John Stephenson
John McCullogh
John Cannon
George Vallandigam
Silas Hedge
David Shepherd   &
Wm. Goe   Gent.
    Ex^d   Ch.

[Page 104]

Norfolk
15th Dec. 1774

George Veal
James Webb
William Atcheson
Matthew Godfrey
John Tatem
John Hutchings
Thomas Veal
Joseph Hutchings
John Portlock
Cornelius Calvert
Samuel Hopper
Goodrich Boush
Malici Wilson   Junr
Matthew Phripp
David Porter
Thomas Newton   Junr
John Wilson
John Taylor   Senr   Quorum
Arthur Boush

Accomack
20th April 1775

Covington Corbin
Isaac Smith
Tully Robinson Wise
John Watts
James Arbuckle
William Silby
Henry Fletcher
William Williams
John Smith
Thomas Teackle   Junr
George Stewart
Walter Hatton   Quorum
David Bowman
Edward Kerr
Thomas Bayly
William Parramore   &
Edmund Scarburgh   Gent.
    Ex^d   Ch.

[Norfolk—Continued]
Bassett Moseley
John Brickell
Robert Taylor
William Smith   and
James Archdeacon   Gentlemen
    Ch.

Norfolk
20th April 1775
George Veal
James Webb
William Atcheson
Matthew Godfrey
John Tatem
John Hutchings
Thomas Veal
Joseph Hutchings
John Portlock
Cornelius Calvert
Samuel Hopper
Goodrich Boush
Malachi Wilson   Junior
Matthew Phripp
David Porter
Thomas Newton   Junior
John Wilson
John Taylor   Senr Quorum
Arthur Boush
Bassett Moseley
John Brickell
Robert Taylor
William Smith
James Archdeacon   &
Humphry Roberts   Gent.
    Exam^d Ch.

[Page 105]

Augusta
Ap^l 20th 1775.
Silas Hart
John Dickinson
John Christian
Daniel Smith
Archibald Alexander
John Poage
Felix Gilbert
Abraham Smith
Samuel McDowell
George Moffett
Sampson Matthews
Alexander McClanachan
William Bowyer
George Matthews

[Augusta—Continued]
Michael Bowyer
Alexander Robertson
John Gratton
John Hays
Thomas Huggart
James Craig
Elijah McClanachan
Josiah Davidson
William Tees
John Skidmore
George Croghan
John Campbell
John Connolly
Edward Ward
Tho⁸ Smallman
Dawsey Penticost
John Gibson
William Crawford
John Stephenson   Quo:
John McCullough
John Cannon
George Vallendigam
Silas Hodge
David Shepherd
William Goe
Alexander McKee
James Innes
Thomas Galbreath   &
William Harrison   Gent:
    Ex⁴ Ch.

INDEX

www.ingramcontent.com/pod-product-compliance
Lightning Source LLC
Chambersburg PA
CBHW060411090426
42734CB00011B/2286